Heart Winds

Finding the Way Home

By

Jeff C. Crawford

Includes "LIFE AROUND THE BURG"

Heart Winds

Finding the Way Home

A story of Healing, Hope and Humor

By

Jeff C. Crawford

Includes "LIFE AROUND THE BURG"

Dedication

I would like to dedicate this book to five people who made a difference in the first thirty years of my life. These life-shapers include my mom and stepdad, Evelyn and Sam Rashbrook, Mom and Pop Harris, Amanda and H. Ray, and my sister, Connie Bielata.

My mom and stepdad, to whom I refer as "Dad" as my story unfolds, loved me and did everything they could to make sure I was on a right and responsible path. Mom had a difficult task, emerging out of an orphanage and then fending for us— and defending us—through half of my teen years, until she found true happiness with my Dad, Sam. Together they worked hard and enjoyed life. They modeled a humor that was infectious and crucial for life. I have attempted to celebrate this in "The Adventures of Sam and Evie." Mom taught all of us many ditties, including this most memorable one: "It was midnight on the ocean, not a streetcar was in sight, the sun was shining brightly, 'cause it rained all day that night, it was summer-time in winter, and the snow was rising fast, and a barefooted boy with shoes on, stood sitting in the grass."

Mom and Pop Harris came into my life when I was twenty-two years old and had found Home in the Lord. Pop was my pastor and Mom was a nurturer. They were my mentors, and I can say that I am who I am today in major part because of the ways they incarnated the Lord of love, forgiveness and acceptance. Like I mention in "Home," they were the core of the fabric of people who shaped my life spiritually. I spent days and nights in their home. There was always a welcome, physical and spiritual sustenance, and laughter. Ten years after I surrendered my life to Jesus, Pop died. Mom lived into her nineties and enjoyed being "grandma" to our first-born, Jed.

My sister, Connie, has been with me throughout life. She is only a year and nineteen days younger than I. We supported each other through some rough times growing up. We also experienced much joy. You can catch this throughout the book. Connie found much happiness when she met and

married Jack Bielata in 1966. They lived mostly around the Jamestown, New York area, and were in our parsonages for visits. For many years we celebrated Christmas together as a larger  family. Jack was only sixty when he died in August 2004. This affected Connie going forward, but she has been able to hang in there with her children and grandchildren so close by. I will forever be grateful for the care Connie gave our Mom after Dad died in 2009 at the age of 82. Mom lived with her in Ashville, New York, until her death on Mother's Day, 2016, at the age of 91.

Introduction

The writing of this book began as a whimsical look at my years growing up around Frewsburg, New York. I wrote several mostly humorous reflections and submitted a few to some of my high school classmates. Their journey down memory lane evoked much joy as they experienced once again the people and events which shaped our lives together during those formative days.

I knew as I wrote that I also wanted to describe some of the adventures, or misadventures, of my Mom and Stepdad, Sam. Dad, as I came to call him, was a hard worker who enjoyed life. When he and Mom married on June 16, 1962, a beautiful thing began to happen. It became apparent to my sister, Connie, and I that two people, each with a great sense of humor, had found each other. They could laugh at mishaps and even entertain us with them.

As I wrote these pieces, pain surfaced. Physical and emotional abuse by my biological father and its effect on my life became an undeniable part of the story. In fact, it was one of the ways these points of focus tied together. This becomes apparent in the reading of the book. What I was writing morphed into something larger. A prequel to my first book, *Bat Tongs and Other Humorous Reflections on Pastoral Ministry*, took shape.

In addition to "Life around the Burg" and "The Adventures of Sam and Evie," there is a description in two additional sections of how I matured and began to experience healing from the abuse I experienced during the first sixteen years of my life. "Belonging to Uncle Sam" provides a look into my years serving in the US Army, and "Home" focuses on my college and seminary days, where I found healing and home as I made commitments to Jesus Christ, pastoral ministry, and Beverly Poe Crawford.

So, this is really a book about the journey of my first thirty years. As the reader will see, a whole gamut of emotions surface as I strive to craft the story of the sculpting of this part of my seventy-three years. I could never write without my significant humorous outlook playing a major role. However, it is my hope that the candid excavation of the damage to my emotions found here, and the Lord's ability to bring about healing, will provide hope for some who read this book.

To Him be the Glory!!   Jeff Crawford, March 2019

Table of Contents

LIFE AROUND THE BURG

THE ADVENTURES OF SAM AND EVIE

And other books by the author.

Life Around the Burg

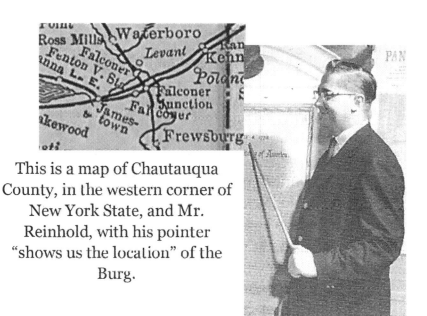

This is a map of Chautauqua County, in the western corner of New York State, and Mr. Reinhold, with his pointer "shows us the location" of the Burg.

On the Move

I was born at General Hospital in Jamestown, New York on August 8, 1945. I like to tell people that I was born "between the A bombs." Those two world-changing events occurred on August 6 and 9. The devastation wrought by these nuclear devices, as unfortunate as it was, saved countless American lives. I came to realize the import of this later in life when my father-in-law told me that he was to be a part of an invasion force of one million men, many of whom would have lost their lives had the war not been brought to such an abrupt end. My wife of 43 years may never have been

born! I am not sure why I arrived at this description of my birth other than it makes something unremarkable seem more remarkable.

When I was about the age of one, my parents and I moved to Shawnee Mission, Kansas. This was done to accommodate my father who was from nearby Missouri and had a job with a company by the name of CO-OP. This company, based in Kansas City, sold feed and other products to farmers. Dad was a career salesman after the war. I wish I would have asked him why he chose his vocation, since he had been raised on a pig farm. He flew PV-1 Twin Engine Bombers in the Pacific during World War II.

His being a fly Boy was how he and my mother met. Because of bad weather, he had to land his trainer in Jamestown, where Mom lived with her sister. She worked at the telephone company patching people through to each other. She was a nineteen-year-old fresh out of the Odd Fellow's Orphanage in Meadville, Pennsylvania. Somehow a date was arranged, and the result was a difficult marriage for mom and the birth of my two sisters and me.

We lived in Kansas for eight years. I have a few vivid memories that include being stung by a bumble bee on my right ear and thinking I might die, living in a new house on Monrovia Road with a huge asparagus field across from us, peeing (for the FIRST... and last time) on the electric fence that stretched across the edge of our back yard, smelling the horse manure on the other side of that fence, my mom and I picking tomatoes off the vine and with a little salt seasoning eating them like apples right there in the garden, and seeing mom argue with my third grade teacher over the correct spelling of my name! The teacher insisted that it should be spelled "Jeffery!"

Oh, and I will never forget spending two weeks each summer at Grandpa Crawford's Pig Farm outside Kirksville, Missouri. Dad always took two weeks off so that he could get back to his roots and help with the farm. The image that stands out the most is standing on the corn wagon with grandpa as he "slopped the hogs." I can still hear him calling, "SOOEY, HERE PIGGY, PIGGY, PIGGY!"

At the end of third grade in 1954, because of mom's homesickness for her family, we headed back to Jamestown. Dad went ahead of us to secure a job and housing and we–mom, my sister, Connie, and I--followed on the train. I can picture mom soothing us as we click-clacked along those rails on what seemed like an endless journey.

Our home for the next two years was "The Projects" on Forrest Avenue. These were low-income row apartments used for veterans returning from World War II. I completed fourth and fifth grade at the Milton J. Fletcher Elementary School while living there. I also joined Mrs. Ailing's Cub Scout Pack, played baseball on a homemade field until dark, got cornered and reprimanded for throwing snowballs at cars, and experienced the consequences for stealing a quarter out of my mom's purse.

It took Dad two years to become financially stable enough to purchase a house on Water Street on the outskirts of Frewsburg, a village five miles southeast of Jamestown. He had established himself as a Prudential Insurance Agent. I was eleven years old when we moved to The Burg in 1956.

Neighbors

Terry and Jerry

We moved to Water Street in 1956, and our house was in the middle of three about a half mile south of the village of Frewsburg. The Mattocks family lived next door, and the Eklunds lived across the street. I didn't remember much else about who lived nearby until I sat down with Terry Mattocks in the summer of 2017 to reminisce. Terry reminded me about Ivan Quaint whom we called "The Bread Man." He was very generous with day-old bread he got from the local grocery store. Then there was a family by the name of Stettler. We called them the "Settlers" because they reminded us of people from the 1800s. They churned their own butter, burned kerosene, and some of their floors were dirt.

I became good friends with Terry and Jerry Eklund. Terry and Jerry were about the same age, something like a year and a half older than I. Our adventures are too numerous to remember, let alone recount, but I will be sharing some of them here and elsewhere.

Summer nights found Terry and I sleeping out under the stars and fighting off mosquitoes. This always involved swapping crazy stories. We never seemed to get tired of the same old ones. We were known to call people randomly and ask if their refrigerator was running, telling them to "go catch it." On one occasion, we called a local radio station and requested a song, saying we wanted to dedicate it to "two of the nicest guys in the world, Terry and Jeff." Since there was a cow pasture right behind our houses, Terry and I occasionally got into "Cow Pie" fights. This involved picking up dried manure and sailing it at each other.

In the spring I would help Terry check his muskrat traps. He always had one or two lines. He would skin muskrats he trapped and sell the pelts for 75 cents ($1 if they were high quality). This led to one of the most hilarious incidents of those early years, involving Terry, Jerry, and I.

One time we found a skunk in one of his traps. We decided to get Jerry since the trap line was behind where he lived. Jerry and his dog, Shep, joined us in deep contemplation about what to do about this. Jerry came up with the insane idea that "this was a young skunk," and maybe we could fool it into letting us spring the trap and then make it into a pet. Even more insanely, Terry and I bought it. Jerry got some rope and tied a loop on end. As Terry and I worked at distracting this "youngster," Jerry tried to creep around behind it so that he could drop the "lasso" over its neck and spring the trap! As you can imagine, things didn't go as "planned" --you might say Jerry got "skunked!" He and Shep got sprayed, and we all took off running down through the field. Terry and I were trying to get as far away from Jerry and his dog as we could.

Reaching home, Jerry's mom made him take off his clothes outside, and she put him a tub full of cold tomato juice. The clothes were left to air out (rot) in a tree, and we had to take my .22 up and shoot the skunk. That night we were all planning on going to the Russell Roller Rink, just over the Pennsylvania line. We recollect that "stinky" Jerry was able to join us.

When Terry started driving, his Volvo became our transportation to school, relieving us from having to either take the bus or walk into the Burg. Terry could find the humor in almost anything. I figure he got this ability from his dad, Julian or "Poody," who was a big kidder. Not long after we moved to our house on Water Street, Poody told me there were moose down by the Conewango. I was pretty gullible and was waiting for him to show me the tracks! I didn't live that one down for a long time. I know that a part of who I am is because of these guys and the friendship we shared.

Terry Mattocks

Jerry Eklund

My Best Friend*

Jerry Westman

My first year at Frewsburg Central School was sixth grade. The teacher of our class was Mr. Poor. He had a goofy sense of humor that often reflected on his name. One day the snow was swirling outside. He stood gazing through a big window that helped form one of our classroom walls. Suddenly, he erupted into laughter and exclaimed, "It looks like it's snowing, but it's... snot!"

I have a vivid picture of the day Jerry Westman's face turned blue when the clip on his bolo tie got stuck against his neck. Mr. Poor had to use scissors to cut off the clasp! It was during those days that Jerry and I discovered that we were two country boys who had much in common. The one thing we didn't have in common was the home life we each experienced. There were stability and humor in Jerry's house. And I found a welcome from his mom, Irma, at the family farm on Carlson Road in Kiantone.

There were a number of ways we could be entertained while at the Westman "estate." Jerry's dad, Bob, kept a couple of horses that we would ride around the area. The only time I got frightened was when we took the horses onto a concrete slab that had been laid for a new National Gas Company headquarters in Kiantone. It didn't take us long to understand that the slipping and sliding they were doing wasn't healthy for them or us.

Jerry had a gizmo that we drove up and down Carlson Road. It was a simple two wheeled scooter powered by a two-cylinder engine. We gained a few skinned-up legs, but, thankfully, in those days of no helmets, we didn't hurt ourselves badly. There were many summer nights when we camped out somewhere on the property and went skinny dipping in the neighbor's pool. That pool was also a gathering place for some of our classmates on those sticky days. Yes, we wore swimming suits!

I will never forget Jerry's mom hiring us to clean out a two story chicken house. $10 each--$5 a floor--sounded like the beginning of a wealthy life, until we began to "dig in." First, we had to use pitch forks to rip up the top layers of dried manure. That was hard enough. Then we reached the putrid soupy stuff underneath and had to find shovels. The pungent odor almost knocked us unconscious!! I can still hear "Mom" Westman chuckling when we described completing one of the worst jobs either one of us ever had. I don't even know if that coop ever got used after that!

I can't count the number of sock hops we attended either at Spencer's Barn or school. One time Jerry's dad picked us up from one of these. He had been drinking, which was a bad habit of his. We remembered hanging on for dear life as he flew up Spencer road slurring, "Eh, a hundred milesh an hour... knock off a couple a telephone polesh, Eh!"

Speaking of driving, Jerry got his permit and "wheels" before I did, and we had some thrills cruising around the Burg and beyond. The "thrills" went too far the night we decided to be cops. Somehow Jerry had "acquired" a blinking red light from a construction site. We rigged it up by attaching wires to a 6-volt battery. Jerry would speed up behind an unsuspecting driver, laying on the horn, while I held the light on the dashboard. We couldn't believe how gullible these people were. They pulled over every time!

It was a barrel of laughs as we flew by stopped cars until we pulled this on the wrong person. The driver we pulled over on that night began chasing us. The pursuers became the pursued. Jerry zigged and zagged all over Frewsburg, finally believing we had lost this "maniac." The hilarity of this night of masquerading turned temporarily into a sigh of relief. After dropping me off at my house on Water Street, Jerry drove home. Upon arrival, he received a rude awakening. Mom Westman was waiting and asked him where he had been. He mentioned driving around the Burg with me. She then told him that Bob Payne, the Frewsburg town cop, had called her. Mr. Payne informed her that he had been returning from the grocery store in the family car and that he had been pulled over by impersonators using a blinking red light! After a chase, he had gotten the license number and it was Jerry's. They agreed that she would take care of holding him responsible.

In school the next morning, I burst into laughter when Jerry told me that our ruse had been exposed, and his mom had taken away his driving privilege for a month. Every time this incident would come up during the ensuing years, Jerry reminded me of my reaction: "You could laugh because you didn't have to bear the consequences!" Then we would both enjoy another comedic incident in our journey of friendship.

After graduation, Jerry and I went our separate ways but always maintained our relationship. Later, after both of us served our country in the armed forces and were married, we helped lead our high school class reunions. To say we enjoyed reminiscing about those days around the Burg is an understatement. I officiated at Jerry's marriage to the love of his life, Elisabeth. Unfortunately, Jerry died several years ago at age 60. I provided the major eulogy at his service, describing to those in attendance some of our shenanigans. A piece of me belongs to my best friend in high school... and beyond.

*I used this title for Jerry's Eulogy.

Gigging Frogs

Almost from the time we moved to our house outside of the Burg, I discovered the wonders of the Conewango Creek. It was not far behind where we lived. I had to traverse a pasture, a field, cross railroad tracks, pick my way through a swampy area full of skunk cabbage and lined by some woods, and there I was, at the brink of excitement. To me, it was misnamed, at least the part of it that I visited regularly. Maybe it was my boyish perspective, but it seemed more a river than a creek most of the time. It was fairly wide, deep and full of carp, bullheads and other kinds of fish, some snakes and flotsam and jetsam in the form of discarded cans, tires and rotting limbs of trees.

My main interest in going to the Creek was in hunting the bullfrogs that inhabited its banks. Somewhere during those years I experienced the thrill of this kind of hunt and the delectability of the legs. I was always looking for the bigger ones, because their legs were more worth the effort. It was fairly easy to find them by listening for their croak but to actually gig one required some stealth. Sometimes I felt like Hawkeye in The Last of the Mohicans as I crept along the edge of the creek with my homemade frog spear. The spear had a metal three-pronged end screwed to an old broom handle. Once I gigged one, I would put it in a bucket I carried. I headed home after I had at least five or six. Reaching home, I would make sure they were dead (usually they were mostly dead), relieve them of their legs, cut off the feet, peel the skin off the legs and either freeze them or prepare them for the frying pan. Some people might compare them to chicken wings, but they had their own unique tastiness.

I must admit to feeling pretty heady about catching, preparing, and cooking my own food found "in the wild." Actually, my sister, Connie, did most of the frying, even  though she had an aversion to these appendages. But a rather hilarious incident took place one day when she wasn't available. My next-door neighbor, Julie Mattocks, volunteered to cook up my catch of legs. I had rolled them in a bowl of flour, and she took over from there, picking up each one and carefully placing them in a frying pan greased with butter. The fun started when the legs began to twitch--almost jump--in the hot pan. Julie screamed at this bizarre spectacle and ran out of our house! I managed to laugh my way through cooking them up. BOY were they delicious!!

Rafting the Conewango

There was a time each year when the Conewango became particularly magnetic. Spring rain and the Chautauqua County snowmelt caused it to overflow its banks and swell to several times its normal size. My thoughts turned to rafting on this creek that had become like a shallow swamp. Only the railroad bed prevented it from consuming more territory.

I loved going down there with my neighbors, Terry Mattocks and Jerry Eklund, to float the rafts Jerry's older brother, Larry, cobbled together with our help. Cliff Nobbs's barn was a treasure trove of stuff we needed--55-gallon drums, bailing twine, pallets and planks--to lash together these floating platforms. Actually, it was typical for there to be some usable pieces of wood floating around as well. At any rate, we managed to haul these creations down to the launch site and somehow, they held together long enough for us to enjoy a few afternoons of feeling like Huck Finn.

Old bamboo fishing poles or limbs cut from partially submerged trees helped us keep our balance as we "poled" around "lake" Conewango. It seemed strange to see fish swimming where normally the ground was dry. The tufts of grass and small trees protruding out of the water seemed always to hold a surprise or two-- a ruffed grouse would suddenly fly up or something else would scare the bejeebers out of us! Occasionally, we would come upon an animal which hadn't escaped the rise of the creek. The carcass would be floating nearby or hovering just below the surface.

I will never forget the time we encountered a dead cow. I am not sure if this was one of Cliff Nobb's heifers or if it belonged to another nearby farmer. Actually, Tallow Hide, a cowhide tanning business on the outskirts of Frewsburg, wasn't too far away. Could it have been? Maybe, but however it got there, and whose ever it was, there it was, staring up at us from its watery grave with glazed over eyes and those big nostrils. It was a macabre sight and makes me think of the Dead Marshes in the Middle Earth of J.R.R. Tolkien's Lord of the Rings. I was only relieved that we didn't end up capsized anywhere near that rotting, bloated bovine!!

This Ritual of Spring will always be an unforgettable part of my life around the Burg.

"Chautauqua" Pond

NOBBS POND TODAY

Local farmer, Cliff Nobbs, had a barn and fields just south of where we lived. Not only did I find work with Mr. Nobbs, but I also enjoyed his property. He had a pond a quarter of a mile or so behind the barn, and it was a focus of fun during those years around the Burg. The only exception to this was when my dad, who had little patience, got frustrated because I would not dive off the old wooden board that extended over the east side of the pond, and decided to throw me in. Well... I guess I "learned" to dive!

The pond was about seven or eight feet deep in the middle and made for a swimming hole as well as a frog home. I didn't gig many frogs there, but you could depend on hearing the chorus of croaks upon approaching. However, there was a point where fish were somewhat in abundance. That's because Terry Mattocks and I decided that we should try stocking the pond. We spent most of a day on Chautauqua Lake catching sunfish and perch. We had a washtub filled with eighty or so of mostly alive fish when we arrived back at the pond, and our little body of water became "Chautauqua Pond."

A guessing game unfolded for the next year or so as to how many of these fish would survive in this small habitat that mostly froze in the winter. To our amazement, some did make it, and we spent some summer nights camping beside the pond and catching a fish or two for our breakfast. We had been Boy Scouts and had our metal cookware ready to go, after we built a fire and filleted the fish. There was nothing like freshly grilled perch to start off the morning. The ingenuity of two teenage guys living in the boondocks still makes me laugh!

I became curious as I was writing this book, wondering if that pond still existed. One day in the summer of 2017, I drove up Water Street and saw a road beside where the barn once stood. It had been torn down long ago and, in its place, stood a tangle of weeds and trees. I parked at its entrance, noting a "Posted" sign. It was quite a walk down a dirt road, involving two bends. As I made the turn at the second bend, there it was, much bigger than I remembered it. In my excitement, I barely noticed someone working on a piece of equipment across the road from the pond. We surprised each other but made quick acquaintance. Dave Bloomquist introduced himself as the owner, and once he was convinced my snooping was innocent in nature (I was dressed in golf shorts and shirt), he was glad to show me around. He explained that he had reconfigured the pond.

I asked him if there were any fish in the pond, and he surprised me by saying that his grandchildren recently caught a good sized perch while fishing off the dock located on the west side. I wondered, "Could it be?"

Woodchuck Hill

Hunting was something I enjoyed during those Burg years. It provided me with another form of escape from the uncertain and sometimes abusive situation at home. Gigging frogs provided some enjoyable hunting adventures, but I actually spent more time hunting varmints with my Single Shot, Bolt Action Savage .22. My dad had insisted that I attend a "Hunter Safety Training Program," and I still have the certificate of competence that certified that I had been given "sufficient instruction in the safe handling of firearms to qualify for a hunting license." I was fourteen years old when this was issued.

I had a variety of terrains and habitats to choose from when I got home from school, and during weekends or vacations. Sometimes I would grab a pocket full of long cartridges and head for the Conewango Creek where carp would surface to sun themselves. They made for easy targets and since they were "junk" fish, I didn't mind eliminating a few. We had a saying that if you caught one and wanted to cook it up, you nailed it to a board, put it in the oven, and when it was ready you removed it from the oven, threw away the carp and... ate the board! Other times I would go into the woods across the road and up the hill and use chipmunks or squirrels for target practice. If I became completely bored, I would find a way to waste a few rounds by

State of New York
Conservation Department
HUNTER SAFETY TRAINING PROGRAM
CERTIFICATE OF COMPETENCE

This is to certify that
JEFFREY CRAWFORD
has been given by the undersigned sufficient instruction in the safe handling of firearms to qualify for a hunting license.
L.C. Roman
Instructor

Date 8/14/59 Title N.R.A.I.

seeing if I could shoot a bottle cap off a stump or ventilate a piece of bark.

My favorite place to hunt was Woodchuck Hill. It was located near Cliff Nobb's pond. It was an amazing mound perforated with woodchuck holes. I could only imagine that a village of those groundhogs lived in this small hill. I first discovered this hill by following my neighbor, Terry Mattocks, there when he hunted chucks. He reminded me in a recent conversation about how he "initiated" me. He told me that bees were nesting in a particular hole and that if I was careful, I could get close enough to see them. As I peered into the hole, Terry fired off a round into a nearby connecting hole. A swarm of angry bees chased me part way home, stinging me several times. Upon seeing me, my dad stormed over to confront "Poody" Mattocks, Terry's dad, demanding to know, "What is the matter with your son?!" Terry's wife, Sue, listening to the recounting of this incident, asked me why I was still his friend. We got quite a laugh out of this one.

Well, when I began visiting this hill for my own hunting purposes, I used as much stealth as I could muster when approaching the target area. The 'chucks weren't always immediately evident, but if I concealed myself sufficiently and waited long enough, one would surface. I only had one shot, so either I reduced the population by one or I headed for the creek or the woods. One of the questions I would like to ask the Lord when I get to heaven is, "Why Lord? Why did you make these varmints?" I'm sure it wasn't so that boys could use them for target practice, or...

Camping Out

One of the things I enjoyed doing during those Burg years was camping out. I had an ideal "site" in a stand of woods across the street from where I lived. On the one hand, it was fairly close to home, while at the same time, it felt like a remote place. I had built a small fire pit and cleared out some brush with my Boy Scout shovel, a sickle, and hatchet. I had a two-person pup tent and always had a friend who joined me for a night or two.

One of these overnights stands out in my memory. A friend named Bill Johnson, who lived in Jamestown, was down for the night. We enjoyed a campfire, accompanied by the night sounds of owls hooting, coyotes crying, and sticks cracking from some always mysterious night prowler. It was a beautiful night to take in the aroma of a wood fire and feel the cool air of the forest. Finally, we turned in. We had no sooner climbed into our sleeping bags than we heard strange noises that included growling. Then we heard what seemed like clawing at the outside of the tent. We were on the verge of being scared out of our wits, when my friend Bill sat up, clutched and raised my hatchet, and yelled words to this effect, "Whoever you are, you'd better be somebody we recognize when you stick your head into this tent, or I'm going to chop your damned head off!!" Through the tent flap came the face of Jerry Eklund, my neighbor who lived just down the hill. Jerry was laughing like a hyena. We all got a laugh out of it, and Jerry was thankful that Bill hadn't decided to swing first and ask questions later.

Another place that made for great camping out was Stillwater Creek. It was located just off Route 60, about halfway between Frewsburg and Jamestown. Guys and girls from the Burg made it our favorite swimming hole. There was a big old tree that arched its branches over a wide and deep place in the creek. Someone had tied a thick rope to one of those branches, and we would swing out over the water, and either do cannon balls, or flip over for a dive. Once in a while, a mud fight would break out until someone got hit in the wrong place.

Occasionally, the guys enjoyed setting up tents on the bank of the creek and spending the night. This was a little harder to supply than camping closer to home, but we managed to bring enough to eat, roasting hot dogs and marshmallows over a campfire with sticks cut and sharpened from a nearby sapling. Night skinny dipping was always anticipated and enjoyed until one night when someone, whose name shall remain anonymous, used the creek as his toilet. We discovered his dirty deed when several of us were swimming around, and someone exclaimed he had bumped into something that felt (and smelt) more like a turd than anything else. When the cry, "SHIIIIIIIT!" went up, we probably resembled mutant albino frogs as we cleared the creek in a matter of seconds! The "poopetrator" was extremely embarrassed that anyone would encounter what he had done and felt so guilty about it that he went to his priest and confessed his... sin!

Camping out always meant adventure, with the possibility of the unexpected, even bazaar, occurring. It was just another piece of colorful thread in the fabric of growing up around the Burg.

"You're going to Jail!"

alloween in the Burg was always highly anticipated. Of course, there were those times when friends and I went door to door trick or treating, but it became more of an occasion for pranks. Many of the pranks were the run-of-the mill, like sneaking up to a porch where a carved out pumpkin contained a lit candle, taking off the top and blowing it out. Once or twice I was surprised by a light bulb instead of a candle! We toilet papered a tree or two and egged a house here and there.

It got more serious when we lit a paper bag containing cow manure, dropped it on someone's porch, rang the doorbell, and then ran like banshees! We were so busy running that what happened afterwards escaped our enjoyment. On one occasion a local farm boy declared he was going to "pave Main Street with a dump truck loaded with cow shit." We all eagerly awaited this ludicrous antic which never happened because he came to his senses.

I never did figure out how a farm implement got put on top of the school building. Generally, mayhem was kept to a minimum, but just to make sure things didn't get too far out of hand, the local police chief, Bob Payne, hired extra help. He "deputized" a few characters, some of whom were known to us "wild boys," and some who weren't. It was an encounter with one of these "deputies" that I remember the most.

It was a Halloween tradition to move an outhouse into the "five corners" where Ivory Road, Institute Street, Falconer

Street, Main Street, and Frew Run Road intersect. I have no recollection of where we got the outhouse, but there it was. It took several of us to carry it up Institute Street. It was difficult to hide what we were doing because of the street lights and other activities that were drawing the attention of those who had been charged with keeping "law and order." But we seemed to be doing an amazing job of concealment. In fact, we felt like ninjas as we moved that one-holer with the quarter moon cut out of its door covertly down the sidewalk.

Just as we began positioning it in the intersection, I was caught in a giant bear hug from behind! A voice growled, "You're going to Jail!" I realized that I had been caught by a big oaf who had been "deputized." My immediate reaction was the thought, "No I'm not!" A burst of adrenaline, brought on by shock and fright, enabled me to squirm my way out of the grip of this "deputy." The distance I put between him and me in a matter of seconds still amazes me. The journey out of the village and up the half mile to my house on Water Street happened in what seems like the snap of a finger. This put the punctuation on a Halloween night that I will never forget!

Learning my P's and Cue's at Kyle and Little's

One of the places I loved to hang out during my teen years was Kyle and Little's. It was mostly known for its eight lane bowling alley but there were other attractions for a "Burg boy" like me.

Upon entering, customers walked between a high counter on the left, where candy, cigarettes and nuts were displayed, and a magazine and newspaper rack on the right. Just past the sweets and smokes, there was a soda fountain with a sitting counter lined with stools. Across from this there were two booths. I would love to know how many hours I spent in one of those booths, sipping on a Cherry Coke and shooting the "jive" with friends like Jerry Westman, Dave Swanson, Candy Olson and Joanne Rice. In fact, Candy Olson Kidder has helped me to picture this part of the inside of Kyle and Little's. While all of this offered enjoyment and intrigue, my obsession became what was found in a side room.

In this room were two mahogany billiard tables covered with deep green felt, with well worn leather pockets. Dual lamps were suspended over these tables. I don't remember how I became so enamored with this game, but somewhere around the age of fifteen, my romance began. As time went on, I was able to sharpen my skills, and I really loved playing eight-ball, nine-ball and pea pool. Pea Pool involved a leather "jug" and dice-like peas numbered from one to fifteen. The "jug" containing these peas was shaken and each player took two. One of these determined the order of play and the other was kept secret and only revealed when the ball it represented was pocketed. Well, you get the idea. More people could play than in a regular game of pool.

All of this went quite well until Kyle, one of the owners, became aware that I was "underage." I believe you needed to be eighteen to play, and I always fell short of that. He was a stickler for maintaining this rule, and I could depend on being told to leave if he happened to be working that day. Little, on the other hand, seemed to look the other way. So, there were times when my play was abruptly ended and, of course, it was very frustrating. During my sixteenth year I was developing my P's (various pool shots) and Cue's... Cue (Stick) "wizardry." I knew how to select a stick that was straight and

decide when chalking was needed. I had learned how to slide it between my fingers for the best accuracy. I also became adept at using a "bridge" when the cue ball was too far to reach for a good shot. I was quite good at picking the right angle to carom balls offside cushions into the pockets.

Meanwhile, Kyle was still kicking me out of the pool room every time he saw me in there with a stick in my hand. Such was life for an aspiring pool shark like me. My skill level reached the point where I could win my share of eight and nine-ball games. And more than once I took my "game" to Jamestown to a pool hall off Second Street. It was always a bit intimidating because I entered this place from a smaller than normal door on the street level, and then climbed down a set of steep steel stairs that spiraled into a dimly lit smoke-filled room with six or eight tables. Over each table hung a shaded light, and there were usually several older guys in T-shirts with cigarette packs rolled up in their sleeves leaning over the tables. I can still hear the CLACK of billiard balls hitting each other both there and at Kyle and Little's.

When I was in Kyle and Little's, I was in familiar and friendly territory, but the pool hall in Jamestown made me nervous. I was afraid that after I beat one or more of those guys in T-shirts, I was going to be taken outside for another kind of beating. But it never happened, and I found myself reveling in my ability to surface out of that "cue cavern" a winner.

Although I rarely played after those high school days around the Burg, my acumen for playing the game of pool has never completely faded. And now that I own my stepdad's prized cue, I occasionally will find a game somewhere and once again test my P's and Cues.

Basketball and Cider

My first love, sports-wise, in high school was basketball. I couldn't wait until classes were over each day during the fall season so that I could focus on basketball practice. I worked hard and was on the Junior Varsity in the 10th grade. I didn't get to play much, but I knew that if I "paid my dues," I would find playing time the following year. I was a starter on the JV team during my junior year and remember scoring the winning basket during a tight game at a rival school. Playing the point on defense, I intercepted a pass and drove to the basket, putting in a layup at the buzzer. My biggest disappointment was that my dad always had something more important to do than watching his son play basketball.

My senior year proved to be a huge challenge! Anticipating serious playing time on the Varsity, I was diagnosed with mononucleosis right before the start of the season. Actually, this was a relief to my mom because the symptoms I reflected seemed to indicate something much more serious, like cancer. But I was devastated. I had worked hard to play on the varsity team finally, and even being kidded about having the "kissing disease" didn't relieve my disappointment. I could attend practices and shoot baskets but was not allowed to run or compete. The coach, Mr. Randall, was nothing but an encouragement during this most trying of times.

Practices (except for my senior year) were exhausting. Red faced and thirsty; we would leave the locker room and head for the cider mill on Falconer Street. The mill could best be described as dilapidated and a bit unstable. It was a three story building propped up on one side by large beams to prevent its collapse sideways. When the cider presses were running, the whole building vibrated, rattling the windows!

The process of making cider went something like this. Mr. Howard, the owner, would dump apples of any and every kind and quality out of large wooden crates or boxes. The apples would be moved up an elevator taking them to a grinder. There the apples were ground into pulp, worms and all. This pulp was then released onto a cloth-covered press rack and wrapped tightly. Several of these racks were prepared, stacked one on top of the other. Called the "cheese," these racks were compressed, using several thousand pounds of pressure. The "squeeze" or juice would flow over the "cheese" and be piped into a holding tank where it could be cooled and filtered one more time. It was quite a process, and one can imagine that with at least two of these hydraulic presses, there was a... whole lot of shaking going on!

Mr. Howard was a memorable character. He was a bit rotund and always wore an apron over a well-worn T-shirt. He usually wore a stocking cap. I was always captivated by the way he worked a growth on his tongue through a gap created by a missing tooth, whatever he was doing. He was not a man of many words, but his generosity was unforgettable.

He offered anyone who was thirsty a cup of ice cold cider from a spigot driven into a wooden barrel laid on its side. We didn't give a thought to the fact that there was only one wooden cup used by everyone! The picture of Mr. Howard with his warty tongue, working in his rickety cider mill, offering the boys from basketball practice something to quench their thirst, will always be a part of the fabric of Life around the Burg.

Old Home Week

Every June around the end of school, a carnival would come to the Burg. It was called Gala Days or Old Home Week. The whole village and the surrounding area looked forward to it because it was full of fun and games. Many towns and villages across America still have something like this.

Trucks would arrive loaded with equipment and in a few hours, up would go the Ferris wheel, Tilt-a-Whirl, Flying Swings, and various Kiddy Rides. Then it wouldn't take long for the games to be set up along a grass walkway. The Ring

Toss, Shooting Gallery and Soft-Ball Throw were always big hits. The High Striker or Strong Man Game was a mainstay, where mostly men tried to ring a bell by hitting a rubber covered lever with a 10 pound Rubber Mallet. A cacophony of

voices would soon be heard, calling customers to these games and rides.

Of course, there were the food and drink concessions. There would soon be "chefs" pulling taffy, dipping candied apples and baking and sugaring fried dough. The smell of French fries permeated the air. The beer tent always shaped up to be a place of mystery from where laughter and boisterous behavior emanated.

I attended Gala Days as much as I could but found that money evaporated, and so, eventually, I was able to find work helping the man who ran the Soft Ball Throw. It was two bits--25 cents--to buy three balls to throw at metal milk jugs. I was the set-up man for the jugs after they got knocked off their perch by guys looking to impress their gals and win them a "prize." I also stocked the prizes, hanging them on the side of the tent. There were little and big stuffed animals and other semi-worthless items that were given to prize winners. If you could completely knock over all three jugs, weighted to make it harder, then you could choose a big fuzzy bear! It was fun, and I made a little coin to spend on taffy or a Ferris wheel ride.

The Strong Man always fascinated me. I never tried it, because, let's just say, I didn't think I was built for it. But I loved stopping by or watching from the game where I worked. Mostly it was guys determined to show how manly they were who swung the mallet to see if they could clang the bell at the top. Once in a while, a farmer girl who looked like she had tossed more than a few bales of hay tried to see how high she could send the slider. The most hilarious spectacle was the occasional drunk staggering out of the beer tent, picking up the rubber hammer, and with a mighty windmill swing, hitting nothing but the pad next to the lever, shouting a slurred expletive!

My two favorite venues were Fowler's Taffy Concession where I would buy some strawberry, cherry, chocolate or vanilla taffy (3/$1) and the Ferris wheel. I loved to ride it at night, look at the lights of the carnival and the Burg and dream of "a kiss at the top" from an imagined sweetheart. That feeling in my stomach as it took its downward turn is unforgettable.

On the last day of the carnival, there was a parade. To us, it was a big deal. There were always several bands, home-made floats, cub scouts and girl scouts carrying banners, clowns, fire trucks, ambulances, veterans marching with flags, cowboys and cowgirls on horses, and tractors belching smoke. The sounds of horns and sirens pierced the air as kids along the parade route scrambled for candy thrown from parade participants.

I can still hear the game owner I worked for calling, "Three balls for 25 Cents... win a prize!" It was a huge bummer when the carnival left town until the next year. The emptiness in my heart matched the emptiness of the fireman's parade grounds where there had been so much "Burg life" taking place. And yes, I was a true "carnie."

Working for Cliff Nobbs

Clifford Nobbs, whom I have previously mentioned, was a noted local farmer. He had more than one business --The Lamp Post Motel was one of them. His wife was my high school Latin teacher. Mr. Nobbs was an industrious man who needed extra help hauling hay into his barn in the summer and doing some of the dirty work year round. Since his barn and fields were close to where I lived on Water Street, I became an easy hire. This, in addition to my eventual lawn mowing business and paper delivery, became decent sources of income.

It's not hard to conjure up a mental picture of maintaining my balance on the hay wagon and being pulled down the field behind the bailer as it relentlessly spit out one bail after another. We tried to make sure the bales were piled in such a way that the wagon would contain as many as possible while at the same time being balanced. We didn't want to head for the barn and have half a load fall off! (This happened more than once and elicited more than a few choice words from us.) This could be hot and sticky work. I would normally wear jeans with no shirt or hat and would have hayseed stuck all over my upper body as well as the rash that went along with hoisting and carrying those twined rectangles weighing about 40 pounds.

The worst part was going up into the haymow and taking the bales from the elevator, tossing them to the place where they needed to be stacked, and then making sure they were tucked into an appropriate slot so that the right configuration was created. It must have been 100 degrees up there on a typical "hay day." I surely could have been called "Hayseed" with the amount of the residue I wore out of the barn.

Another job I had was cleaning out the gutter in the barn. Mr. Nobbs had no modern equipment back in that day. Some of it hadn't been invented, and he was too small a farmer to have had it anyway. The routine was pretty simple but dirty and stinky. I shoveled manure out of the gutter, stretching the length of the area where the cows were stanchioned, put it into a wheelbarrow, and dumped it into a manure spreader backed up to the outside of the barn. On the occasion that the cows were in the barn, I had to be aware of the possibility of being kicked or splattered. Nothing like this happened, but I did get whapped on the side of the face by a manure caked tail a time or two. The dumbest thing that happened during these "manure operations" was the day I displayed my naivete. It was the first time I rode out with Nobbs to spread it on a field. Something didn't work right at first and the spreader wouldn't throw manure. So, I volunteered to walk along behind to... watch it!

I felt good about all of this farm work, because not only did it make me some money, but it kept me in touch with my pig farming roots. This experience helped cement my identity as a... country boy.

Jobs

In addition to working for Cliff Nobbs, whose barn and fields were a stone's throw from our house, I had two other jobs that provided me with badly needed spending money. I mowed lawns and delivered papers for the Jamestown Post Journal.

Mowing lawns went well, until I mowed my own. I'll get to that in a bit. Most of my customers were older folks who would pay me $5 to mow so that they wouldn't have to do it themselves. In most cases physical issues, including frailty, prevented them from taking care of this task. Normally they supplied me with their own mower, so I could ride my bike or walk from our house on Water Street into the Burg and get the job done. On at least one occasion I did the best I could with an old fashioned reel mower. It brought back memories of having to push one of these around our yard, and let's just say I detested it.

My dad expected me to mow our lawn, and if he were around would always lecture me about being careful and "not hitting anything!" Honestly, he made me nervous as he worked on the car in the garage or in his office in the house ready to explode in anger if he heard the mower hit a rock or run over some sticks. I will never forget the time that dad was lurking as I mowed the front yard. Suddenly, there was an awful clanging and banging. I had run over a steel meter cap! It was grass high and I just hadn't remembered that it was there along the edge of the yard. The mower came to a smoking stop, and my dad launched himself out of the garage in a rage!

I took off running in fear of being manhandled. Well, it turned out that I bent the blades up so they looked like the ones you see in a mixer or food processor. Since I kept my distance, I believe Dad took out some of his frustration as he wailed away straightening them out with a hammer.

My other job involved paper delivery. I had a route in the Burg that extended down Falconer Street to the village limits and included a few other houses on side streets. It was an afternoon paper, so I could deliver after school. I had a bunch of really nice customers, but there was always one thing that frustrated me. I had a few who seemed to never have the money when I came around for the bi-weekly subscription payment. I probably heard every excuse in the book, including a rat ate my $5, or whatever it was at that time. Just kidding, but there were some pretty wacky reasons, and, of course, it left me with less spending money and made me return, sometimes again and again.

I felt bad for one little old woman who lived in a ramshackle house on Falconer Street and just never seemed to be able to pay me on time. Her name was Iva Fisher, and her house was one of the spookiest places I've ever encountered. It was set amongst overgrown shrubs and old half-dead trees, and it was reported that she held séances there. More than once she invited me to come in. I ended up sitting at her dining room table listening to her tales about a dead husband who visited her at night and communicated with her through spirit writing. On one occasion, she took a piece of paper and a pencil and wrote a "message" he was conveying to her from the spirit world. That might have been the last time I spent much time in her house, as if the home and property weren't frightening enough! Maybe that's really why so often she "couldn't pay me." She wanted someone's ear she could bend with these bizarre tales!

As I look back, I am thankful for those small jobs that helped me be more independent and enabled me to enjoy a few games of pool and some sodas at Kyle and Little's, buy a couple of gallons of gas for Jerry Westman's car, and in general enjoy life around the Burg.

Swany

One of my high school buddies was Dave Swanson, whom I have mentioned in a reflection or two. We developed a friendship beginning in the ninth grade. We had some things in common. Dave lived on the edge of the village like I did although I was a half mile out. We shared a hardscrabble mutual existence. And we were both goofballs. At one point, Swany and I had an ongoing chess tournament. Whenever time permitted, I would walk to his house after school and we would play a game or two. This continued for a year or more. I don't remember who "won."

He was one of the classmates I hung with at Kyle and Little's and at Julia's Restaurant. Julia's was a favorite of many in our class. The wall that is pictured in a photo taken in 1962 for our '63 yearbook looks exactly the same today, fifty years later. It is now known as the Dinner Bell. Next to Jerry Westman, Dave was the classmate with whom I spent the most time. Tennis was a part of this.

Swany and I played doubles on our tennis team. We worked hard and had an excellent coach by the name of Mr. Rhodes. I can remember practicing in rain and snow as we prepared for the season. Our familiarity and comfort with each other facilitated the communication and strategy needed to be successful. We were good enough that in both our junior and senior years we represented Frewsburg Central in the sectionals. Our junior year we were runners-up to the Chautauqua County Champions. Once again, in our senior

DAVE AT OUR 25TH HIGH SCHOOL REUNION

year, we made it to the finals, but were defeated by a team from Fredonia, a much larger school.

I can't even calculate the hours Swany and I spent helping to put together a pagoda for the Senior Prom. Our class spent a couple of hours dancing around and through it, but it was a work of art. And he also was one of the guys who camped out at Stillwater Creek. I describe one of those campouts in another reflection. Dave was among several of my friends who called me by the nickname, "Crawd." He wrote this in our senior yearbook, addressing me by my nickname, "Best of luck in everything you do, which will be little since you're so damn lazy. I still say the Navy is better than the Air Force. Here's hoping we take a trophy this year. Why how can we miss with a partner like me?" Well, as indicated above, we almost did just that. I burst into laughter every time I read this.

I kept in touch with Swany after high school. He went on to serve three tours of duty in Vietnam as a Navy Man. He asked me to officiate at his wedding in 1973. I had, just months before, been ordained in the United Methodist Church. I have to admit to being nervous, but I managed to help him and Elaine Ingerson become Mr. and Mrs. David Swanson on September 1, 1973. It was to be the first of at least 150 weddings I would perform over the next thirty-six years as a pastor.

He was a deputy in the Chautauqua County Sheriff's Department, and Elaine was a hairdresser. I will never forget him telling me about stopping someone who was driving too far below the speed limit. We had a good laugh over that one and I am sure he was as gentle as he could be in advising this individual to "speed it up!"

The last time I saw Dave was at our 25th FCS Class Reunion in 1988. He was no longer with Elaine and enjoyed his beer and cigarettes. We had a great time reminiscing. He died in June of 1991. Swany was another one of those special personalities who make up the tapestry of my life and who helped shape who I was to become.

At the Sock Hop

Dancing became a source of joy and release during those years around the Burg. Sock Hops were the rage. There was nothing like kicking off my shoes and gliding around those worn and sometimes polished wooden floors. The birth of rock and roll occurred in the 1950's, and by the latter part of that decade, I was often twisting and spinning my way through life.

CANDY AND I IN THE YEAR BOOK.

The Frewsburg Central High School Gym and Spencer's Barn became the two main venues for my dancing exploits. People came up with all sorts of dances: some that resulted in spastic movements like the "Jerk"; some that involved movement by the legs and feet only like the "Mashed Potatoes"; some that caused one to prance like the "Pony"; some that used swimming motions like the "Swim." There were others that had one "Twisting" and still others that involved the whole body moving like the "Jitterbug." Then there were dances

INSIDE THE BARN

where couples did the "Stroll" between lines of guys and gals facing each other. My sister, Connie, was one of my main dance partners. There was no intimidation or fear of embarrassing myself, although Connie claims that I was sometimes embarrassed to dance with her in public. After all, she was my sister. We could practice at home, and since she was just a year and nineteen days younger, we were both at most dances. But there was also the closeness and romance of slow dances. I was always looking for that someone who would put their "head on my shoulder." And it seems like every evening ended with the song by the Overtones, "Good Night Sweetheart."

I remember the well-known Buffalo disc jockey, Tommy Shannon, from KB Radio, coming to our little burg and spinning music for one of our sock hops. My dancing accomplishments were noted in the 1963 Yearbook when Candy Olson Kidder and I were voted "best dancers" in the Senior Class.

My favorite music is still 50's and 60's rock and roll. Thankfully, it still enjoys popularity. Danny and the Juniors were proven prophetic in their 1958 top twenty hit, "Rock and Roll is Here to Stay." My wife and I have enjoyed dancing those dances over the years, and we have talked about how dancing provides a great metaphor for our relationship and even life. As partners there are times when there is a seamless flowing through life's twists and turns but then there is the inevitable stumbling and the need to start over. The contrast of space and intimacy, energy and rest, reflected in dancing, is so much a part of the nature and need of all of us.

The Unforgettables

Our teachers at Frewsburg Central School all made some sort of impact on our lives. In a sometimes-indiscernible way, each one shaped who we are. It's easy to remember some of these personalities from high school with their distinct traits and idiosyncrasies. Many times, it makes me laugh to picture them in action.

I think of at least five of these shapers of my life whose teaching styles, combined with their personalities, made them unforgettable. This "Hall of Fame" would include Carol Nobbs who taught Latin, Clyde Deeks, who taught math, Victor Reinhold, who taught history, Doug Randall, who taught biology, chemistry and physics and was the Varsity Basketball Coach, and Cliff Bowman, who was our English teacher.

I did not enjoy Latin, but for some reason I thought I had to take it. It was probably because languages, even dead ones, were viewed as important to one's complete education, and after all, my goal was to earn a Regent's Diploma. Mrs. Nobbs was the wife of Cliff Nobbs, for whom I worked. I remember her as an older teacher who looked like an old-fashioned schoolmarm. She was determined that we learn enough Latin to be able to understand Julius Caesar and his culture. I can't begin to number the times I got spoken to for not paying attention. I do remember one line from Caesar: "Veni, Vidi, Vici." It means, "I came, I saw, I conquered." So, I guess I learned something memorable in her Latin class. I have repeated this line on rare occasion when I have overcome in some circumstance. She was much beloved by all of us, and we dedicated our senior yearbook to her. She signed my copy with these words: "I have missed your merry presence very much in my classes this year. May you have much success in your life."

The math classes taught by Mr. Deeks were some of the most mind-numbing exercises in futility I have known. I admit that I hated this part of the Regents curriculum and felt that it was quite useless. This is not to say I didn't benefit in some way from working on all those algebra, geometry, and trigonometry problems. I guess it sharpened my thinking skills heading into the future. I somehow managed to "C" and "D" my way through this morass. But I was so bored that I apparently found it most exciting to provoke this generally mild-mannered man. At least this is what my classmate, Conrad Donelson, has told me since, and even demonstrated. Conrad, who was an "A" student, seemed to eagerly anticipate my goading Mr. Deeks with absolutely inane comments and responses. Apparently, I kept this up until he detonated like a stick of dynamite, screaming, "I'VE HAD ENOUGH OF THIS AND WILL TOLERATE IT NO FURTHER!! DO I MAKE MYSELF CLEAR?!" Thinking back, I feel badly that I harassed such a well-meaning and gentle soul who was just trying to do his job, but I can't help but laugh. Lord, forgive me!

Victor Reinhold was probably the most facially expressive in his unleashing on us all kinds of historical tidal waves, tidbits, and trivia. It is impossible to forget the way he scrunched up his face and pursed his lips when he told us about "every other house in Virginia City being a house of prostitution." And he delighted in pulling down maps and charts and slapping them with his pointer as he made sure we knew about this or that historical cataclysm. Even though I only remember the one nugget about Virginia City, I know that Mr. Reinhold tried to drive home the fact that it is crucial to learn from history so that we don't repeat the mistakes of the past--or something like that!

Doug "Josh" Randall (we called him "Josh," after Steve McQueen's character in Wanted, Dead or Alive, a TV series at that time) in some ways appeared to be a ticking time bomb. Maybe it was just that he was wound a bit tight. He was an intense, no nonsense disseminator of insight and could deliver some serious wake up calls if one wasn't paying attention! When he clenched his teeth, and his jaw bone became defined you knew it was time to get with it. I have a vivid recollection of Mr. Randall reaching the boiling point with a wiseacre classmate in biology class one day and abruptly taking three giant steps up the levels of the lecture area of the lab, grabbing this student by the lapels and lifting him out of his chair. He let him know without any doubt that he would not tolerate disrespect! On another occasion, he saw me mindlessly touching the American Flag hanging in the gym for some patriotic occasion. Suddenly I heard, "Mr. Crawford, how would you like to write a thesis on the American Flag?!" Actually, Mr. Randall was a good teacher and coach. And he was one of the few adults at that time who I felt believed in me, especially as my basketball coach.

Finally, there was Cliff Bowman, whom we affectionately called "Bowinkle." He was fresh out of college and began teaching high school English at FCS during our junior year. He brought a lot of creativity into classes. He had us deliver speeches and write about very ordinary things, like paperclips.

He also had Lance Barker and I stage a fight in class for a writing focus. I think our classmates were utterly shocked the day we began an argument that escalated into a desk shoving, shouting, and wrestling match. We both received "A's" for doing something that came easily. It was pretty clear to everyone that we were not what you would call buddies. I credit Mr. Bowman for being a formative inspiration as I went on to hone my creativity and skill as a preacher and writer.

These are five "Unforgettable," who were amongst the bouquet of life-shaping personalities in life around the Burg.

Mr. Randall and Mr. Bowman at our 25th High School Reunion

My Alma Mater

I felt... and still feel, a certain attachment to the school where I was educationally and socially shaped during my years growing up. I have been back a couple of times since graduation, and each time I stood gazing down that locker lined hallway where I entangled my life with people whom I will never forget --teachers, classmates and others I hung with. Those "others" were comprised of friends from classes above and below. Frewsburg Central was a small school --our class fluctuated depending on the year (there were 46 senior pictures in the 1963 Yearbook, *Senior Leaves*).

SCHOOL HALLWAY

I was involved in chorus in the junior high.

I still find myself belting out lyrics from "Spanish Cavalier," quickly followed by "Solomon Levi."

However, I didn't last too long as a chorister, but somehow ended up in the band. Our leader through junior high was the legendary Arthur Goranson.

He had played a key role in the establishment of the New York State School Music Association and the Jamestown High School Band. I remember being intimidated when I had to take cornet lessons from Mr. Goranson, but I knew people were grateful that he had come to our little community and school to spend the last years before retirement. I played in the brass section of the band and on occasion shared in a solo trio at a concert. But doing anything that involved standing out made me so nervous my lips would quiver--not good for playing an instrument with a mouthpiece! I just didn't have a lot of confidence after being told since infancy in one way or another by my dad that I didn't measure up. I drove my sister up a wall with my horn blaring at home when I practiced. I mostly enjoyed being in the band and lasted until the very end of my senior year. I will tell that story in another reflection.

I have mentioned some of my teachers elsewhere. I was not what anyone would call a good student. I had a hard time concentrating whether in study hall or at home when studying. I remember being brought to my knees by the Future Farmers of America--or Ag--Teacher, Mr. Zimmer, when he got tired of my fooling around in study hall. He made me stand up, squeezed me in the shoulder just below my neck with his big strong hand, and down I went. I got the message, but it was still hard to accomplish anything meaningful in this setting. Sometimes I picture myself as clowning my way through Junior and Senior High. And I graduated with a cumulative grade average somewhere south of 80. I had almost miraculously managed to pass all the state tests (Regents) except for one, which apparently didn't prevent me from receiving my diploma stating that I had earned a "Regents Diploma" designated "Scientific."

I loved sports involvement. I believe my slight success helped me salvage some confidence and more of a positive self-image. My three sports were tennis, track, and basketball. All of the coaches, but particularly Mr. Randall, my basketball coach, did nothing but encourage me. I invested myself in these and was rewarded by an enduring sense of accomplishment.

I was shy when it came to dating. In fact, I would describe my love life as completely underwhelming. My first date was with Cindy in the eighth grade, and we were chaperoned. My dad actually drove us to a dance and then made sure Cindy arrived safely back at her home. Then I have a vague memory of planting my first kiss on Phyllis, with whom I was briefly infatuated. Finally, I managed to take Phyllis and Julie, my next-door neighbor, to the junior and senior proms. I can think of a classmate or two whom I would have loved to get to know beyond friendship, but the ones whom I thought were most attractive weren't interested in an immature and awkward guy like me. I resonated with the Beatles song, "Nowhere Man."

A highlight of my school days came when I was given a prominent role in the junior play, "A Hillbilly Weddin'." I played the part of Obeey Upschlager who marries Ceelie Belsnickle, the dirtiest, homeliest hillbilly girl in the valley.

About the only thing I didn't like about those school days was an odor that permeated the classrooms during the warmer part of the year. There was sometimes the distinct smell of something dead wafting through the open windows. It came from the Jamestown Rendering Plant on the outskirts of Frewsburg. It was also called Tallow Hide, and it was where cow hides were tanned. I could never figure out why if it was named the "Jamestown Rendering Company," it couldn't be located nearer Jamestown!

When it came time to graduate, I hated the idea of leaving my Alma Mater. It was a place and people where I felt accepted and secure. Now I had to go into the big bad world and make my way. I took friendships, memories and the school song with me and have them to this day. In fact, as time has unfolded, I have become the primary force for keeping our class of 1963 reunions going. We have them every year since our 50th. And I still find myself singing these words:

Where templed foothills proudly rise,

And right and honor rule,

We lift a song that never dies

For Frewsburg Central School.

Our will to stand where glory calls,

Shall pride and honor bring

To Alma Mater, in whose halls

Our sweetest mem'ries cling.

Senior Picture

Zero for Band

(Written with input from my "partner in crime")

This is a story begging to be told involving life around the Burg. As I mentioned elsewhere, I was a cornet player in the band. We had plenty of brass but were drummer- deprived. That is with the exception of Dennis McKeever and one or two others. Denny was the primary snare drummer and was critical to preparing concerts full of marches. During our senior year he and I were involved in a most unfortunate turn of events.

These events occurred one Saturday in June, nearing the end of the school year, as we took part in an All County Music Festival in the three thousand seat amphitheater at Chautauqua Institute. But before I recount this tale, I must tell of another. It was some months prior and happened in a gym class.

Our gym teacher, Mr. Schofield, had the class participate in the Rope Swing. Each student was to run out, grab a heavy rope suspended from the ceiling, swing out and when swinging back, at the top of the arc, let go and drop onto a mat. Denny, the drummer, would not participate because of what had happened the year before. He had ended up on his butt!

Well, Jerry Westman called him a "coward" for refusing to engage in the "swing." His manhood questioned to the breaking point, Denny, at the end of the class, grabbed the rope and launched into a mighty swing. The rope twisted as he swung back and he prematurely let go before it reached its apex. Off balance, he fell backward, bracing with his wrists underneath. He broke both wrists!! Jerry and Bob Hussey helped him to the nurse's office. On the way, Denny, who also could be called "Mr. Shenanigans," groaned loudly that he had broken both legs!

Arriving at the hospital, his mother almost fainted when she saw him walk into Emergency holding his... wrists. For the next month he had his right hand out of commission and had to use a rubber band around his left wrist and hand cast to somehow play a drum! Months later all was healed, and it was time for the next shenanigan. This one involved me.

As I mentioned at the beginning, this involved a most unfortunate turn of events. Denny and I had both had been selected to play in the All County Band that was to be a part of the Music Festival at Chautauqua. This concert, made up of students from schools throughout the county, took place in the early part of June and always began the season at this legendary venue in the western part of New York State.

It so happened that on this same Saturday, our Varsity Baseball Team was scheduled to play in the sectionals at Jamestown's Minor League Stadium. We desperately wanted to be at the game, believing it our duty to beat drums and blast "Reveille" and the "Cavalry Charge" to rally our team. The game started at noon and would last at least two and a half hours, but we had an afternoon practice that began at 3 pm. If the timing was right, it left us barely enough time to travel back the twenty miles along the west side of Chautauqua Lake, from Jamestown to Chautauqua. We had another critical decision to make involving transportation, since we all were supposed to ride the school bus.

Ah hah! Dennis, who drove an old Volkswagen bus, would "miss the bus" and thus have to drive to Chautauqua. Mr. Stearns, our band instructor, was not pleased but accepted Denny's excuse of oversleeping when he arrived separately for the morning rehearsal. Our skullduggery almost worked to perfection. We broke for lunch, drove to the stadium, did our thing for our team, and headed back to the amphitheater. With only about a half hour window, we got hung up by weekend traffic which we hadn't thought about, and we arrived late for the practice. Denny remembers walking down the aisle to the stage in the amphitheater and seeing Mr. Stearns on the conductor's podium with the main maestro. It appeared that we were being glared at and that everyone was staring at Denny. He had a drum solo in one of the songs, and that may have made our entrance more conspicuous. At any rate, we failed to take into consideration the fact that Mr. Stearns was lurking around the amphitheater making sure all his students were accounted for. It's those little details that get us into trouble when trying to be devious.

On Monday morning, the PA system blared for all to hear that "Jeff Crawford and Dennis McKeever are to come to the School Superintendent's Office." Goosebumps from the 1,000-member combined choruses, band and orchestra playing and singing "Faith of Our Fathers" to conclude the All County Music Festival had barely faded. Now, shaking in our shoes, Denny and I feared what might occur. Sure enough, ushered into the office by the secretary, we encountered both Superintendent Robert Murray and Mr. Stearns. Mr. Stearns asked us why we were late for the afternoon rehearsal. We were honest and told him where we had been. Putting that together with Denny's "need" to drive to Chautauqua, it was obvious to him that we had been deceptive and "broken his trust." We were stunned when he announced our penalty. It was at the end of the school year and about all that was left was for us to turn in our books. In addition, this was an extra-curricular activity! "How bad could it be?" we wondered.

Since Mr. Murray thought it important that an example be made of us so that no one would "try something like this again," we were to receive a zero for the band--for the year!! Neither of us wanted something like this on our final report card in high school. We were pretty broken up about it then, and only time has enabled us to laugh about the whole debacle. Every once in a while, I drag out my report card from a file I keep and see the word, "DROPPED --in red letters-- printed in the fourth marking period. (Mr. Stearns probably chuckled at the thought that anyone looking at our high school grades, who might have something to do with our admittance to college, could ask us, "What about this word 'Dropped' in red? Does this mean you got a... zero for band??")

Part of the band—Dennis and I are in the back row, second
and third from the right as you look at the picture

Coming to Faith

At some point during those years living on Water Street, our neighbor Jerry Eklund invited my sister Connie and me to the Sunday school and church services where he attended. We accepted, and as time went on, the Weidler Memorial Evangelical United Brethren Church in the Burg became our church home. Jerry, being older than I, had a car and would drive us to the church and back. The Sunday school class I was in was made up of guys around my age. This was during the late 1950s and early 1960s when it was typical for even teenage boys to be in church on Sunday. Religion was valued in American culture. Our teacher, Mrs. Phillips, was a sweet woman who was determined that we learn something about the Lord Jesus Christ. She must have been a saint to put up with the shenanigans that we pulled. I can attest to the influence she had on my life.

The Rev. Arthur Vrooman was the pastor, and I remember being impressed with his leadership and preaching. There was a choir every Sunday, and the worship service was not boring. I went through confirmation and became a member of the church. Every year there would be some sort of evangelistic emphasis. This usually involved a traveling preacher coming to town and holding revival services. The church had a strong culture of people coming to personal faith in Jesus Christ.

I would say that during those years, I acquired some sense of faith. On one occasion I responded to the invitation of an evangelist, made my way to the altar rail in the front of the sanctuary, and kneeling, gave my life to the Lord. But faith became white hot for me during the viewing of a film that portrayed Jesus dying on a cross. I was suddenly overwhelmed by deep sorrow and began weeping as I observed his agony. I didn't understand the whole sin thing, but I didn't have to. I just KNEW Jesus died for me. The impression this made on my life proved inescapable.

The issue during these teen years was that outside of that context, I had little encouragement or modeling of how faith should be lived out. My parents had little interest in church, and with the upheaval in my home, I eventually drifted away. But the Lord had gotten a hold of me, and though I would be unaware of his presence and influence for several years, He had me in his grip.

Dad... to Stepdad

I referred to my dad's failings in prior reflections. For whatever reason, from early on, I became his whipping boy in a literal way. I remember mom telling me about how spilling milk while sitting in my highchair could earn me a slap across the head. In fact, on one occasion my grandparents were visiting our home in Shawnee Mission, Kansas, and one of his out-of-control slaps earned a stern reprimand from Grandpa Crawford. Even the old humorless Missouri pig farmer knew dad had crossed a line.

It got worse as I grew into my teen years. I mentioned how I ran away from dad after I hit the steel cap with the lawn mower. I had learned that in his rage there was no telling what physical pummeling might occur. Along this line, there is a night I will never forget. I had locked the doors, believing that dad, who had the habit of being out late, had a key. At around 2 am I was awakened by his pounding on the door into the house from the garage. I stumbled out to unlock it and was met by my furious, alcohol-fueled father. He chased me into my bedroom and repeatedly pounded on me as I lay sprawled across my bed on my stomach.

It became clear as I progressed through my teen years that Carl H. Crawford, Jr. was a browbeating, intolerant man for whom it was his way or the highway. And his obsessive-compulsive behavior paired with excessive drinking made it virtually impossible for anyone to really like him, let alone live with him. Mom endured his bullying for as long as she could and finally had to find a safe space. She moved out when I was fourteen years old, taking our youngest sister, Paula, with her. Thirteen year old Connie and I were left to navigate the emptiness. I will never blame mom for this. I didn't understand it at the time as much as I did later. But I sensed deeply the abuse and deprivation she had experienced. I say "deprivation" because dad would not provide the money for her to buy clothing and food for us on many occasions. Mom was a great baker and seamstress, so we had the best she could create even during these times.

Mom felt so guilty about leaving Connie and me that she came back a year or so later and tried to make a go of it. But dad's persistent drinking combined with his unrelenting badgering led to a second exit with the promise that she would somehow rescue us from this situation. That happened by the time I was sixteen. Mom met the man who became my stepdad, Sam Rashbrook. They were married in June of 1962, and we joined them, a stepbrother, Doug, and our sister, Paula, in Jamestown on Barker Street.

I had been able to escape the emptiness and abusiveness of the home while living with dad, but Connie was trapped and expected to do many household chores, even ironing dad's work shirts. While it was a relief to be united with mom and our baby sister, I had an adjustment having a responsible male figure who expected me to be accountable. My life was suddenly more circumscribed. I also was extremely distressed about not being able to spend my senior year at Frewsburg Central. Well, my new "dad," Sam*, and mom worked out a deal with my high school English teacher, who lived in Jamestown. Mr. Bowman agreed to pick up Connie and me and take us to school each morning. It was a five or six-mile drive. Since dad still lived in the school district, there was no problem with this arrangement. Sometimes we rode home with Mr. Bowman, but other times I would hitch a ride with friends, or my stepdad would come and pick me up from activities like basketball practice.

So Life around the Burg continued through graduation, even though I was a bit farther away. I will be describing my stepdad further in later chapters. Let me say at this point that I was already experiencing his commitment to us as a dad, and I loved his sense of humor.

*My step-dad, Sam, also had the nickname, Bud. Mainly close friends and family used this name. I referred to him as "Bud," for the first few years after he and my mom were married. At some point after I was separated from active duty in the army, in my middle 20's, I considered him as my "real" dad and began to refer to him as such.

The Adventures of Sam And Evie

Wedding Day

40th Anniversary

Transition

Things moved rapidly during the summer of my graduation. My stepdad owned a home in Bemus Point, along the east side of Chautauqua Lake. He had been renting this home for several years. He had arranged for the renters to move out and for us to begin living on Harold Avenue. He had built this two-story house. There were two bedrooms upstairs that were configured so that you had to go through one to get to the other. Connie and Paula had the bedroom at the top of the stairs and Doug, and I occupied the other. It was a bit awkward, but we managed to make it work with an occasional battle between Connie and me involving throwing each other's clothes all over our respective bedroom floors.

Since I had absolutely no inclination to attend college, I found a job at the Super-Duper Grocery Store on Fluvanna Ave just north of the city of Jamestown. It was a ten mile drive to work from where we lived. My wheels were a '57 Chevy that I had been able to purchase late in my senior year. It wasn't long before I acquired a one-of-a-kind 1963 Lincoln Coup with two yellow racing stripes across the top. It was given the name "The Black One," but this is a story for a later chapter.

I worked part-time at the store for the better part of a year. I was a stock boy, a bagger, and I assisted folks to their cars with groceries, as well as shagging carts from the parking lot. A high school classmate, Gary Lobb, also worked there, and we have many nutty stories of food fights in the stock room and other goofball behavior, including helping ourselves to a few cherries from jars on the shelves! It was during working hours that I remember hearing about the assassination of President Kennedy on November 22, 1963, announced over the store PA system. We had to join a union in order to work there, and this became a source of extreme frustration when someone with less seniority was promoted to full-time over me. Thaddeus was related to the office bookkeeper, and I witnessed my first instance of nepotism.

Actually, this had the positive effect of motivating me to seek other employment, and my stepdad got me a job where he worked as a foreman. I became a piece worker at Blackstone in Jamestown, checking radiators for leaks as they came off a line. As time went on I knew this was not how I wanted to spend my career. So, I went to the local Army Recruitment Office and inquired as to what job I could get if I enlisted. This began the process of my spending three years in the U.S. Army as a Motion Picture Photographer, which I will write about later.

Backyard of home on Harold Avenue in Bemus Point. Doug, Mom and Paula, with the back end of the 1953 Lincoln in view.

The Bemus Boys

It was in the summer of 1963 that Connie, Paula, Doug and I settled into our "new" home on Harold Avenue in Bemus Point. Connie, a senior, was soon busy adjusting to a new school. She seemed to fit in nicely, making the cheerleading squad. She had been a cheerleader for Frewsburg Central, and here she was doing the same thing for Bemus Point High School.

One of the things I got busy with was building a tree house with my brother, Doug. There was a perfect tree in our back yard with sturdy limbs that enabled me to anchor it solidly. It had a trap door for entrance from a ladder below, a window and two bunk beds for sleeping. I was pretty proud of it, and it turned out that it was so well built that dad had to use a chain to pull it out of the tree a few years later when it fell into disuse and the tree began to show signs of rot.

I also discovered a group of guys with whom I could hang out. They were a year or two younger than I, still in high school, but I resonated with their focus on enjoying life. They all had nicknames. There was Tinker (Tink) or Bozo (Boze), Teabags (Bags), Leeburg, Gus, Shep, Brownie, Yentz and Ricey. These monikers were derived from either using a version of their last name or something they were known for in childhood. The fact that I was given a nickname was an indication that I was accepted as one of the boys, even though I was a "new kid on the block." They called me "Freaker," because I had the habit of overusing that word in one way or another.

We spent many an hour, mainly on weekends, playing basketball in Tink's driveway, riding around Chautauqua Lake or Jamestown in Ricey's car or mine, hanging out at a place called the Casino in Bemus, attending dances at the Midway Park Roller Rink, and doing other things too numerous to remember. Several of the Bemus Boys starred on the football, basketball, and baseball teams for the high school. And since my sister was a cheerleader, I enjoyed attending these events. It was at that time that a New York State record was established for the success of these major sports programs.

A highlight was joining several of the guys at Leeburg's house to watch the Beetles arrive in New York City in February 1964. We engaged in a lot of harmless craziness like flying down seasonal access roads in the middle of the winter, plowing through fender- deep snow. Somehow, we managed to make it through without becoming hopelessly stuck in a snowbank. Ricey loved to pull these antics. I was driving one night in Jamestown when, for entertainment purposes, I deliberately drove the wrong way on a short one-way street. It almost ended in big trouble when we were stopped and quizzed by a police officer. I completely fabricated my response, telling the officer that I was unfamiliar with Jamestown and had missed the sign.

While in Bemus, I acquired a most unique set of wheels, mentioned in the previous reflection. Tink wanted to sell his 1953 Lincoln two-door sedan, with its unique racing stripes. I needed a car and bought it for $600. I could only open the hood enough to change the oil and put antifreeze in the radiator. The car we dubbed "The Black One" became a main source of transportation for the Bemus Boys. We were religious about throwing our beer cans in the trunk. When I went into the army in November 1964, I left The Black One parked at home. A few months later, dad told me that the bottom of the trunk had given way and all those cans fell out in the driveway creating a mess he had to clean up.

SHEP, ME, GUS AND TINK

It is amazing that I lived in Bemus for a total of fifteen months and was able to form such a close bond with the Bemus Boys. In the summer of 2016, I attended a memorial service for Norm Rice--Ricey, who had died earlier in the year. Always the adventurer, he had spent his career as a pilot, never married, and kept two homes, one in Bemus and the other in Florida. I spent some time with Bob Shepherd--Shep, Bob Gustafson--Gus, and Ray Head--Tink who had helped organize the service. I got the biggest kick out of Tink reminding me of the nickname the Boys had given me and sharing his impression of my "disappearance." He said, "You were here one minute and... you and The Black One were gone! I always wondered what happened to you and that car!!"

Sam, My Dad

I mentioned my step-dad, Sam, in the first section of this book, "Life around the Burg." Now I want to flesh out this unique man who I learned to call Dad. * Sam and my Mom met through a group called, "Parents without Partners," in Jamestown, NY. Both longed for someone to complete their lives and help provide their children with that missing parent.

Dad had served in the U.S. Army at the end of World War II and was working at Blackstone Corporation in Jamestown. He worked in the radiator and heater division of this company where they supplied parts to Chrysler Corporation and other car and truck operations. He had been married previously and had adopted two children with his former wife. The divorce settlement involved each spouse keeping one child. So, when mom and dad were married on June 16, 1962, Doug, his son, along with the three of us, helped to form a five member blended family. This began a 47-year journey of love and joy.

I remember things being a bit tough at first. Not only did Connie and I move out of our Frewsburg home, leaving everything behind except for our clothes, but I needed to adjust to having a responsible father figure. More than once I exploded at my new dad, Sam, that he was "NOT my dad!" He took all of this in stride, providing us with as much practical love as he could--he was present, helped put food on the table,

offered counsel if he could, and drove to the Burg countless times to pick me up from basketball practice or some other extracurricular activity

I believe his character was most profoundly reflected in his adoption of our younger sister, Paula. Paula was born in April of 1956, just before our move to the Burg. She experienced the upheaval and uncertainty in our family as a little girl. Dad sought to help her know stability and give her the fatherly love that had been missing in her life. Sometime in 1965, Paula's last name was legally changed to Rashbrook. His utter commitment to loving her as his daughter was powerfully evident through the ensuing years as she pursued self destructive paths, particularly involving alcohol. ˟ ˟

Dad brought something else into our life together--humor. He had a wacky sense of humor that complimented my mom. Together they made quite a pair and could engage in some major hilarity. Even something that was accidental, or not intended to be funny, could end up becoming a comedic incident. I will describe several of these in following chapters.

But I must mention here a couple of examples of nuttiness that illustrate Dad's way of entertaining our family. The first was when he propped up a large headless doll in a chair, positioned himself behind it and made it look like his head belonged to the doll. He pulled this one to prank our sister, Paula, who was probably three or four at the time. A number of years later, he had our little ones, Jed and Jeanna (Joy hadn't arrived at this point) sit in front of the kitchen stove. He told them to be prepared to see a "show" inside the oven. As they stared at the open window, he turned on the oven light to reveal stuffed animals he had placed on the racks!

Dad was a hard working man whose lunch bucket was

packed every morning in time for him to punch into work at 7am. During his forty-two years at Blackstone, he climbed the ladder of responsibility from piece worker to foreman to superintendent of the day shift in the Radiator and Heater Division. During these years he took on a new family and always found ways to enjoy life. I learned to love and appreciate this man who came into my life when I was sixteen years old--Sam, who became my Dad.

From here on distinguished from my biological father.

**My sister, Paula Sue Rashbrook, died on January 22, 1998, due to alcohol abuse. She is pictured above with mom. She was 41 years old. I conducted her funeral service using an exquisite glass serving bowl she had given us one year for a Christmas gift. It had gotten chipped at some point. I spoke about how this bowl illustrated her life, finely etched and transparent, but flawed--like most of us. Mom and Dad always felt like a permanent gouge had been made in their hearts. We all believed that peace had finally come to our loved one who never found safe harbor in this life.

"Little Orphan Evie" *

T he world is full of "insignificant" people – "little" people – who have great influence in shaping life. My mom was one of these persons. In fact, I suspect that most moms are in this category.

According to an Application for Admission to the Odd Fellows Orphanage in Meadville, Pennsylvania, Evelyn Belle Zimmerman was born in Ridgeway Township, Elk County, Pennsylvania on March 2, 1925. She was the sixth born of eight children--one of three girls--to Harvey and Katherine Zimmerman. (The eighth, Glen, died in infancy.) Her mother was a "housewife" and her father was a Lease Man. He worked for the oil and gas industry facilitating the leasing of land for the drilling of wells.

Mom's dad, Harvey, died at the age of thirty-three with heart valve complications. She was three years old and her brothers and sisters ranged in age from thirteen to one. Her thirty-one-year-old mom, Katherine, was left with such a small monthly compensation ($75) that she could not support seven children. Because my grandfather was a paid-up member of the Independent Order of Odd Fellows in Ridgeway, admittance to their orphanage in Meadville became an option.

At first, four of seven siblings were admitted. The two youngest, one-year old Norman and mom, remained with my grandmother. The oldest, Arminta, was ineligible because she was thirteen. Eventually, mom and Norman joined their older brothers and sister to make a total of six Zimmerman children in the home.

At the time of her entrance into the orphanage, mom was the youngest of 103 children. In a May 1929 copy of "The Pioneer," an orphanage publication, there is a picture of mom with four boys with a caption that includes the following: "The little girl is our baby and her name is Evelyn Zimmerman. She is the only girl who doesn't go to school, for she is just four years old. She loves to sing and maybe will sing for you when you come to see us."

Being "put on parade" for those who came to visit became a regular part of life in the home, especially for the "biggest family in here"--the Zimmerman kids--Richard, Wilbert, Alverta, Harold, Norman, and mom. Mom found that embarrassing to experience as she matured, as well as to recollect. But the home depended upon donations, both monetary and material. In fact Donation Day was a huge event. The Home Kids presented a program and sang this song to the tune of "Happy Days Are Here Again:"

"Donation Day is here again, let us sing a song of cheer again. For our cellar shelves are full again, Donation Day is here again." Needless to say, "new" clothes meant newly donated.

Mom was a "lifer." That is, she came into the home at the earliest admissible age and left at age eighteen. Over the duration of her stay, three different couples served as administrators. One can understand the need to be highly organized and to maintain discipline with approximately 100 children in the home at any given time. But this took the form of an uncompromising harshness. Any kind of parental love

and warmth was sadly lacking. When the kids came home from school, they prepared for supper and afterward sat at the table for one hour whether they had homework or not. A bell signaling bedtime rang at 7:30 for the younger children and 9:00 for the older ones and they were to be in their beds. A night nurse patrolled the hallway.

Mom remembered having "cockroach stomping contests" in the bathroom and an "Alteration Lady" sneaking a needle and thread to her so that she could make dolls out of scraps of clothes. One of the cooks taught her how to crochet. In 1933, when she was eight years old, her mother, who was thirty-six, and who she had visited for two weeks in July, died in November of pernicious anemia. Mom remembered attending the funeral service, driven from Meadville to Corry, Pennsylvania, in a "black shiny car."

As mom came into her teenage years, living in the home became even more difficult. In high school, students from the orphanage were referred to as "the home kids." It was extremely embarrassing to be delivered or picked up from school in the black "Home car." The kids walked as much as possible but knew that being late was taboo. There was a woman who sat in a window overlooking the entrance to the home who kept a record of the exact time of arrival. A tap on the glass would indicate that an explanation was due for being two or three minutes late. Dating was almost completely prohibited. A home kid could not say "yes" to an offer. Mom remembered the administrators "flying into a rage" when she was sixteen because a boy sent her a dozen roses.

So, it was with great joy and relief, and probably with some trepidation, that mom was released from the home when she was eighteen years old. Her sister, Alverta, married and living in Jamestown, New York, offered mom a place to live while she got adjusted to life outside the proscribed confines of the orphanage. She got a job at the telephone company as an operator. It wasn't long before she met the flyboy, Lt. Carl H. Crawford.

Addendum

 Meadville School report cards through mom's senior-year, never signed by a parent but stamped by the Superintendent and few photos until her senior picture – the absence of baby and childhood pictures - say volumes about institutional surroundings until she was eighteen. This is a major reason why my sister, Connie, our stepbrother, Doug, and I, were determined to keep her from spending her last years in a nursing home. Thankfully, Connie was able to have mom in her home until her last month of life. She died on Mother's

Day 2016 at the Heritage Green Rehabilitation and Skilled Nursing Facility near Jamestown, surrounded by all of us.

*Written using a combination of documents, notes from conversations I had with mom about her life in the orphanage, and input from my sister, Connie.

***

"You picked a fine time to leave me... loose wheel" ***

I begin the adventures of Sam and Evie with events--or mishaps--that occurred on or near the property that dad was given by his mother, Erma Barrett, in 1965. It was close to 100 acres and included both woods and uncultivated fields located in Ellery Center, NY. This is the same piece of property that Dad gave to Connie, Doug, and me in the 1998. Whatever and wherever it happened, we could depend on Dad and Mom's great sense of humor surfacing.

On this property there was developed a family campsite. I use "developed' loosely, maybe "evolved" would be more accurate. However, it is described, my dad, brother- in- law, Jack, and his son, Jeff, had important roles. First there was an old school bus that served as sleeping quarters with a fire pit for enjoyment and cooking. Eventually the school bus was removed, and a platform was built. This platform morphed into a pavilion and then a cabin. A truck-bed camper was brought in by Jack and used prior to the platform/pavilion being made into a cabin. A later improvement involved an outhouse—a one-holer--being constructed. Mom and dad also owned a small camper, which they brought to the campsite during the summer. It was destroyed in a fire that consumed their garage one year.

All of this was possible because a road had been cleared from the entrance to the property off Haynor Road to the campsite. There was always a need for a brush hog, something to keep the weeds and grass down and to remove small trees and bushes. Dad maintained some kind of tractor up there with a mowing machine attached. I say "up there" because this property was several miles into the hills from their home along Chautauqua Lake. It also acquired the name, "The Boonies."

Water was always a problem when spending any length of time up there. This was eventually solved when dad secured a 55 gallon fiberglass drum and installed a spigot. The only challenge was transporting that drum, filled with water, up to the property and into the campsite. At issue was how to keep something that heavy and unwieldy on the trailer that dad had made to haul stuff to the boonies and elsewhere.

This usually worked without a hitch (no pun intended). Dad would put the drum onto the trailer, wedging it between 2x4s and securing it with a harness that he had fashioned so that it would not roll. Then he would fill the drum using the garden hose. It was a fairly easy task to then roll and slide it off the trailer at the campsite. Only once was there a problem with the stability of the drum. I will describe this later.

There WAS a mishap with dad's handcrafted trailer. Mom and dad were transporting various supplies, including the drum full of water, up to the campsite on one occasion. My sister, Connie, and her husband, Jack, were following in their car. They were just rounding a curve as they drove up Dutch Hollow Road when the wheel on the left side of the trailer came loose from the axel. Connie and Jack watched in horror as the momentum of the detached wheel took it down into a family's yard. There were several cars in the driveway and a number of people had gathered for a picnic on the lawn.

Someone screamed as they saw the wheel careening towards them. Connie and Jack never saw a group of people scatter so fast!

Meanwhile, dad and mom were dealing with the sudden scraping of the trailer axle on the pavement. It didn't take long to discover its cause. They pulled over and were soon apologizing profuscly as they retrieved the renegade wheel from the people's lawn. Thankfully, Jack and dad were able to reattach the wheel while everyone, including the picnickers, enjoyed a huge laugh.

*The title is taken from twisting the title of a song, "You picked a fine time to leave me, Lucille."

**Unlike the other sections in this book, this section is not to be seen as strictly chronological. As the reader can imagine, these stories cover a period extending deep into Mom and Dad's 47 years of marriage.

This seemed like the appropriate place to put tales that needed to be told. These adventures occurred during the time they lived in Greenhurst, another Chautauqua Lake community between Bemus Point and Jamestown. They had sold their home on Harold Avenue in Bemus in the late 1960's.

The Bus

Dad Grilling

It Was A Chainsaw

Mom and Dad enjoy staying in the boonies for a night or two. I mentioned previously that there was a period of time when they kept a small camper up there during the summer months. The campsite off Haynor Road in Ellery Center became a great place for the whole family to gather. I got up there as much as I could once my army days were finished, and I became a college and seminary student. Dad loved to clown around and make us all laugh, like the time he hung a camp stool from his head and pretended like it was normal.

After Bev and I were married, we spent time in the boonies, pitching a tent and spending a few days. When we had our children, camping there became an annual event around the Fourth of July. We progressed from a tent in the pavilion to a popup camper. The family would always gather for the 4th. Not only would we light off fireworks, but dad would bring his homemade cannon and we would fire it, seeing how loud we could make it by packing it with a charge and wad. Of course, the guys all found this hilarious and especially when dad's sister's husband, Al, retorted with shotgun blasts! (They lived on the property near the road.)

The woods on the property offered firewood in abundance. Dad supplied wood for the fire pit at the campsite, as well as for their wood burning stove in Greenhurst. He would sometimes take his chainsaw up to the campsite and disappear into the woods, cutting down a tree and then hauling out the cut logs while mom sat by the fire or in the camper knitting.

On one occasion Dad was gone an especially long time. Mom was beginning to worry when dad emerged from the woods with a piece of what was once his chainsaw. He was pretty shook-up, and mom was upset. He announced: "THIS is what is left of my chainsaw!" He recounted what had happened. He was almost ready to fell a tree when it began to turn on the stump. The chainsaw got stuck and dad took off running, not

 knowing how the tree was going to fall when it came off the stump. Thankfully, he was able to get out of the way, but the tree trunk came straight down onto the dislodged chainsaw, smashing it to pieces!

It didn't take too long for this to become another hilarious episode in the adventures of Sam and Evie.

Intersection Hijinks

For several years my sister, Connie, her husband, Jack, and their three children lived in Greenhurst, where mom and dad lived. This made it handy for Jack to join Dad in developing and supplying the Ellery campsite--the boonies. It also made it easy for dad to pull shenanigans on the Bielata family. The most infamous was a prank Dad unleashed one Halloween. He concealed himself with a mask and long coat and banged on their door. Carrying a garbage bag, he grabbed the bowl of candy Jack had in his hand when he answered the door. He emptied it into his bag, pushed his way past Jack, and headed for the refrigerator. When he opened the door, and began putting bottles of beer in his bag, Jack doubled his fist and declared, "Take that mask off and I'd better know you when you do!" Dad immediately unmasked and both burst out laughing.

Well, they both could be pretty silly, especially after consuming a couple of cold ones. This reached its apex one Saturday after dad loaded his trailer for a trip to the boonies. Jack had walked over and helped fill the drum with water. They headed up Greenhurst Avenue, made the turn onto Route 430, which runs along the east side of Chautauqua Lake. It was only a quarter of a mile until they reached Dutch Hollow Road, which would take them into Ellery Center. It was this intersection that proved problematic.

A rather sharp left hand turn resulted in the water-filled 55 gallon drum becoming dislodged. It rolled off the trailer and into the intersection. Fortunately, dad and Jack felt the shift of weight, and what had happened was confirmed in the mirrors. They were out of the van Dad used to pull the trailer in a New York minute! They soon discovered that they could not lift the drum--it was too heavy and unwieldy. Meanwhile, traffic began to stop and back up as people gawked at this spectacle. The intersection was partially blocked as they tried to horse this run-away drum out of the way.

All of this caused Dad and Jack to begin to laugh like hyenas, and I am sure there were other onlookers who found this hilarious. They finally realized that the only way to get this drum back into the trailer was to drain the water out of it. So, as they howled, the longest ten minutes of their lives expired. And of course, this went down in family lore as another uproarious adventure in the life of Sam and Evie, even though mom was nowhere near this "drum-dump." Their adventures were enlarged to include another family member, Jack Bielata!

On Fire!

Mom and dad kept a neat home and property on Pearl Street in Greenhurst. The house was painted regularly until they invested in beige siding. There was a breezeway that connected the house to the garage. There was a small apartment over the garage that was used by my step-grandmother, Irma Barrett, for a period of years. Thankfully, it was vacant when a fire erupted one night and the garage, their car, and the small camper used by Mom and Dad in the boonies were destroyed. The cause was a small boat motor dad had stored in the garage that leaked gas, ignited by the pilot on a stove. Some of the siding on the house melted and had to be replaced because of this fire.

This was not the only problematic fire that occurred on the Rashbrook property on Pearl Street. As I intimated above, everything had its place around the house. I mentioned in another reflection how Dad would go to the Ellery Property and cut down trees to supply wood for the stove in the house. One could depend upon seeing a neatly stacked cord or more of the wood Dad had split somewhere in the backyard. The hose was meticulously hung on the side of the house. Sometimes lawn chairs were set up so that Mom and Dad could enjoy the back yard in the summer. Mom loved to hang clothes outside, so she maintained a clothesline behind the house.

Along a well-kept chain link fence that corralled their dog, there was always quite a garden. Mom especially loved to grow onions, tomatoes, beans and cucumbers. I can remember as a boy going into our garden wherever we lived and picking a tomato, which mom would wipe off and salt and we would eat like an apple. A ritual of spring was Dad tilling the garden to prepare it for a fresh batch of vegetable-producing seed. This ritual went haywire one spring.

Dad was using his new tiller along the back edge of the garden, which was always longer than it was wide. He got too close to the chain link fence and some of the tines caught. In an instant it began climbing the fence! The machine was hot, and as gas spilled out of the tank, it burst into flames. Dad's immediate reaction was to try yanking it off the fence. About this time Mom saw what was unfolding from the kitchen window. As she stood in front of the sink with the window open, she screamed, "SAM, DO YOU WANT ME TO CALL THE FIRE DEPARTMENT?!"

Dad yelled back, "NO I DON'T!!" He was already on his way to the side of the house to get the hose. He managed to douse the flames and get the tiller off the fence, but it was ruined. They could laugh about it afterward and chalk it up to another adventure of Sam and Evie. And Dad was thankful he had been saved the additional embarrassment of the local volunteer fire department showing up!

The Admiral

Probably the capstone in the adventures of Sam and Evie was what happened on one snowy winter's night in Greenhurst. Mom and Dad were returning from one of their favorite places, the War Vet's Club in Fluvanna, about two miles from where they lived. They typically went there on a Saturday night, enjoyed some drinks with friends, and played a few games of shuffleboard. When they left on this particular night, it was snowing hard. As they drove down Greenhurst Avenue, Dad faced white-out conditions. Pearl Street, where they lived, was a block off Chautauqua Lake.

Creeping along, Dad drove past Pearl Street and past a street that ran beside the lake, thinking he still had not reached the point where he should turn left. There was a launching ramp for boats that ran into the lake, and down the ramp Dad went, making a left hand turn at the break wall. As he slowly rolled along beside the wall, on the frozen lake, in the blinding snow, the front end of the car dropped through the ice and water began seeping into the car. Mom screamed that they were "IN THE LAKE!" Meanwhile, Dad was trying to figure out what to do. The water was only two or three deep that close to the shore, and so after prying open the doors, they got out and managed to work their way back to and up the boat ramp.

They trudged home through the snow, their feet and legs soaking wet. Their only alternative was to call for a wrecker to come and tow the car out of the lake. It took an hour or so before the tow truck arrived, and as the driver surveyed the situation, he broke into uncontrolled laughter. It became less funny when he had to figure out how to attach the winching cable under the back end of the car. Laughter ceased when he had to submerge his hands and arms and got a face full of that freezing water. Uttering a few choice words, the driver finally fished the car from the lake. What Dad feared the most happened when a small article appeared in the Jamestown Post Journal with the title, "Car winched from lake." The next time he entered the War Vets, he was greeted with, "There's Captain Rashbrook!" I am not sure he ever lived that down.

I have entertained countless people with these stories over the years, but this became the funniest of the adventures of Sam and Evie for me to tell. When I told this particular story to a parishioner friend of mine in one of the churches I served, Mark broke into laughter and announced that he was giving Dad a promotion from Captain to Admiral. One of my favorite photos shows the grin Dad had across his face when Mark congratulated him on his "promotion."

When Dad died in August 2009, mom asked me to lead the service but told me that under no circumstances was I to share THAT story. I understood why she felt that way, and I had to honor her wishes, but I was frustrated. I still made some general reference to "The Admiral" while focusing on some of the other adventures and, of course, lifted up Dad's wonderful ability to laugh at himself and enjoy the humorous side of life.

Our family has surely been blessed by the adventures of Sam and Evie. And, yes, the winds of the Spirit have blown through our lives because of having such wholesome and loving parents.

Photo: Mark "promoting" Dad.

Trainee!

One of the best decisions I ever made was to pay a visit to the Army Recruiter's Office in Jamestown, NY. In the early fall of 1964, I introduced myself to the local recruiter and told him I was seriously considering enlisting. We chatted a bit about my journey since graduating from high school and about the probability of being drafted. My enlistment would involve a three year commitment rather than the two year expectation of a draftee. After asking him about job possibilities, he presented me with a large notebook, which I took into a small room to examine.

I was amazed at the options. Glossy page after glossy page described training to be this or that type of technician—radar specialist, weapons handler, aircraft maintenance man. Nothing interested me until I read about being a motion picture photographer. This was something that had never entered my mind, and suddenly here it was in front of me, a boy from the Burg. As I read about the three-month training, it seemed excitingly doable. The Recruitment Officer told me that whatever I chose, if I graduated from basic training, I would be guaranteed to attend that school.

Early that November, I headed for Buffalo, where I went through the legendary physical exam. Yes, thirty or so young men were asked to strip down, form a line, bend over and spread our cheeks. Other than allegedly checking for hemorrhoids, I expected that this was to be our first of many humiliations over the ensuing weeks to break us down in order to form a whole new identity. On November 13 I boarded a bus headed for Fort Dix, New Jersey, my head swimming with questions that both filled me with anxiety and anticipation. The six hour trip gave me plenty of time to ponder the certainties and uncertainties of the new life I was beginning. Eight weeks of basic training was supposed to make me into a soldier, qualified to handle an M14 Rifle, crawl through a field lined with barbed wire under live fire, throw hand grenades, fight hand-to-hand, and do all of the other things a soldier was meant to do in the U.S. Army. Most importantly, it was to shape me up so that I could be part of a seamless whole, an integral part of a combat unit, able to perform my role for those who depended upon me.

The questions swirling in my head had amped up by the time we pulled into Fort Dix and were deposited at a set of barracks deep in the bowels of the base. As I stepped off the bus, I was met by a drill sergeant barking orders that went something like this: "Welcome to your new life, TRAINEE! You no longer belong to mommy and daddy--you belong to Uncle Sam--YOUR ASS belongs to ME!! So, line up over here and you'll be escorted to the building where you will be issued your clothing and other necessary items."

And so, it began. I was no longer "Jeff" or "Crawd" or "Freaker" or whoever. I was a TRAINEE in the Army of the United States of America. Thus, would begin a three year and nineteen day chapter of becoming a man, shaped by a life no longer mine. I belonged to the government and would learn what it was like to be accountable to something way beyond my control and whim.

Man-Making

The first three weeks of basic went well enough. I found myself on the second floor of a two-story barracks in a long room, with two rows of simple steel-framed bunk beds. I was assigned a bed, along with a footlocker and a wall locker. The footlockers, boxes made of wood, were kept at the foot of each set of beds. The metal wall lockers were positioned between the beds. Anything that could be folded went into the footlocker: underwear, socks, and fatigues. My boots and shoes, hats, jackets, and dress uniform belonged in the wall locker. Days began at 0500--5 am. Lights were unceremoniously flipped on, and cold harsh words were spoken to "hit the floor" while reveille blared all over the base. We were expected to be at the company assembly area in front of the Company Headquarters by 5:45, ready for exercise and inspection. Orders were given for the day, and we were dismissed for breakfast.

The rest of the day included activities to challenge and strengthen us physically, plus instruction regarding everything from how to maintain acceptable hygiene to survival skills in a combat zone. After watching a film graphically displaying mouths full of rotten teeth, I realized the importance of proper teeth brushing. We marched and sometimes double-timed (jogged) out to various ranges so that we could become marksmen in using an M-14 rifle and proficient at other aspects of warfare. Double-time was always good for getting warmed up on those frigid Fort Dix mornings, but it was no fun to then, upon arrival at a range, stand or sit while we were instructed. Lunch was brought to us in large field thermoses, or we ate rations like some would later eat in Vietnam.

A trainee never referred to a rifle as a "gun." I remember more than one time when a member of my basic training company had to run around the perimeter of our assembly ground, holding his M-14 in the air with one hand and using his other hand to point first at his rifle and then at his groin, all the while chanting, "This is my rifle, this is my gun, this is for shooting, this is for fun."

In that almost theatrical atmosphere, humiliating someone was par for the course. It was entertaining to find some vulnerable soul to pick on. After all, young men from all sorts of backgrounds were put together for this military immersion. The draft was on, and there were college graduates as well as farm boys fresh out of high school.

A farm boy on our floor had the habit of collapsing into bed and falling fast asleep, with all the lights on. One night the rest of us agreed to prank him by turning off the lights for five minutes and then flipping them back on, pretending to get up and calling out "Reveille! Reveille! Hit the floor!!" It was 10 pm and our gullible fellow trainee got up and began to get dressed as we all broke into laughter.

As I said, things went well enough until one morning during that third week when I was hand walking a horizontal ladder. As I swung from rung to rung, there was a point where I apparently aggravated an old injury to my right shoulder. Hanging all of my weight on that shoulder, my arm dislocated. I still remember it being the most excruciating pain I have ever experienced. I was immediately taken to the base hospital and found relief when a medic, seeing my agony, manipulated it back into my shoulder joint. It was diagnosed as a separation, and I was put in a sling for four weeks.

I stayed with my unit while I rehabbed my shoulder but could not continue training with the rest of the men. I was told that I would have to be "recycled," which meant starting basic training all over again. The most demoralizing part of this was I was left wondering if the Army would keep its promise to me to attend Motion Picture Photography School. I was nearing the end of my month of rehab when the Christmas holidays arrived. I was cleared to take a leave of absence so that I could spend this time at home with my family. I will never forget what happened at the end of this leave.

I had made arrangements to take the train from Jamestown to Newark, New Jersey. Something happened with the train schedule, which in turn messed with my bus ride from Newark to Fort Dix. I knew I was going to be late returning to my company. To say I was shaking in my boots is an understatement. I walked into company headquarters expecting at the least a severe reprimand. Instead I was greeted with something like this: "Glad you are back--now report to duty." I have never forgotten that act of mercy in the darkness of dread.

Basic Redux

After the Christmas Holidays of 1964, at the beginning of the new year, I was in Basic Training all over again. I was once again assigned to one of the old wooden barracks on Fort Dix. It was in the heart of winter, and these buildings, which were heated with coal, were not particularly warm at times. But we were young, being toughened up to be G. I.'s--ground pounders--and so we accepted this as part of the normal fabric of a trainee's journey.

I remember that I occupied a top bunk in this second go-round because of what happened within that first week. I had put my footlocker on my bed so that we could clean the floor in preparation for inspection.

As I reached up to put something into the locker I sneezed, dislocating the shoulder I had spent four weeks rehabbing. It was then, for the first time, that I had to manipulate it back into place. Part of the sickness I felt was because I realized that the rehab hadn't worked. I determined that I would keep this quiet and somehow complete Basic. For the next seven weeks I managed to hand walk the horizontal ladder, crawl under barbed wire, with live fire overhead, and meet all of the other physical demands without another dislocation.

There were several other memorable experiences that occurred during those eight weeks. Men from varied walks of life had been thrown together, with the expectation that the "mixing machine" of basic training would produce a blended whole. Well, one of the guys on our floor came from a home life where personal hygiene was apparently not a priority. We noticed after a few days during that first week that he didn't take a shower daily like the rest of us. Not only did we not see him in the shower, but his body odor became intolerable. After several conversations and warnings, several of us took him, fatigues and all, and threw him into the shower, demanding that he either wash up or else.

Once during that recycle, I pulled CQ (charge of quarters) duty. I stayed up all night to "guard the front entrance." It was one of those military exercises emphasizing the importance of security. It involved sitting at a desk with an occasional check of the coal burning stove. More than once I had to stoke it with a shovel full of coal. I would have been in trouble if the company headquarters building was cold when the staff arrived the next morning. This was where I experienced using evaporated milk in my coffee. There was always a can of this next to the coffee maker, and I found that it added a unique and pleasant taste. Over the years I have occasionally raised a cup of java, flavored with PET or Carnation Evaporated Milk, to commemorate that all-night experience at Fort Dix during basic training.

Deep into basic we had to march out to a range to throw our one and only live hand grenade. It was a frigid morning, and we arrived sweaty after a march punctuated with double-time. On the way, we called out the well-worn cadence that began with, "I don't know but I've been told," included, "Your grandma wears combat boots," and ended with, "Sound off, one two, sound off, three four, sound off, one two three four, SOUND OFF!" Our 50-year-old drill sergeant, who had been doing this for way too long, lined us up in rows and then told us to "bend over and put your head as far back between your knees as you can." Some of the trainees actually tried to do this but many of us half heartedly made an attempt, figuring he was joking. Sure enough, he then said, "Now jump through your ass!" He thought it was hilarious. The rest of us? Not so much. Maybe his motive for pulling this was to loosen us up in case we were afraid of handling a live grenade. My only explanation for remembering this ridiculous incident is the inexplicable nature of my warped sense of humor. Maybe I should blame it on my mom.

Graduation from basic finally came after three months, and I was assured I was headed for Fort Monmouth and Motion Picture Photography School. I was promoted from a Trainee (Private First Class) to Private Second Class.

Motion Picture Photographer

I was on my way to Fort Monmouth, New Jersey, the home of the Army Signal School, on April 2, 1965. It was located 50 miles south of New York City and five miles from the ocean in Monmouth County. According to a document describing its focus, published in the early 60s, Fort Monmouth "offered courses in audiovisual procedures, communications security, data communications, radar systems maintenance, satellite communications, and radio communications."

The Army had fulfilled its promise to send me to Motion Picture Photography School, in spite of being recycled in basic training. This included spending three weeks in a holding unit at Fort Dix until the next fourteen week school was to begin at Monmouth. I was brimming with excitement as I settled into a large brick dormitory on the base. It didn't bother me that once again I was assigned a bunk bed in a bay that accommodated more than thirty soldiers. Like basic, there was an interesting assortment of personalities, which included draftees--two year soldiers--and men like me, dubbed Regular Army, who had volunteered for three years. But here, because of the unique technical training available, there were also men from other branches of the military as well as foreign troops.

More than fifty years later, I still roll my eyes as I picture a particular draftee sitting beside his radio almost every night, tears rolling down his cheeks, listening to Bob Dylan sing "Like a Rolling Stone" and other songs. Dylan's voice, less raspy then, somehow provoked a sentiment that this G.I. couldn't contain. Then there was a brash Marine who proclaimed that "Vietnam isn't a war, it's a brush fire that will soon be extinguished." We all know how that went. I also became friends with a soldier from South Korea, a Sergeant Lee. There was also what seemed like a cadre of Mormon draftees. I was struck by their patriotism, which led them to determine to be the best they could be.

The fourteen weeks of school were filled with practical experiences. We spent much time in the classroom, but also many days all over the base with our 16-millimeter Bell and Howell motion picture cameras. These were windup cameras, and the 100 feet of film always seemed to run out too quickly. I never imagined the details involved in effectively using and maintaining these small cameras. The highlight of my training was being loaded onto a bus for the fifty mile ride into New York City so that we could tour the Army Pictorial Center in Astoria, Long Island City, in Queens. It was a historic studio containing stages where the legendary Rudolph Valentino, star of the 1920s, had made movies. At that time, it belonged to Paramount Studios, before they were moved to California. The Army had purchased it in the 1940s and converted it into a place where training and information films were made. We watched a film being made on a sound stage and visited a building where film was processed. Overwhelmed, I day-dreamed on the bus ride back to Fort Monmouth about the possibility of being assigned to the Pictorial Center. I also thought about how unlikely this was, since it was rare that cameramen were needed there. Our school graduated 20-25 photographers every fourteen weeks, and they tended to be assigned to bases around the country or sent to be combat photographers in Vietnam.

It meant so much to me that mom and dad came to visit one weekend before I graduated. We spent time at Asbury Park, New Jersey, and ate in a couple of wonderful restaurants. They brought their typical laughs, reminding me that no matter what happened following successful completion of Motion Picture Photography School, no matter where I was sent, I was anchored by a home full of love in Bemus Point, New York.

With Sergeant Lee in 1965

A Dream Realized

As one can imagine, it was with much anticipation and some anxiety that I awaited orders for my assignment out of Motion Picture Photography School at Fort Monmouth. I completed this training with my class by the end of June 1965. I began receiving a series of orders on June 25. I was to "tread water" for a month until I had further direction. Early in August my destination was made clear. I was being sent to the place I had dreamed of, the Army Pictorial Center in Astoria, Long Island City, in Queens! I only had to travel 50 miles north to New York City. A short bus ride took me to the "base."

I use "base" loosely because the buildings comprising the Pictorial Center occupied three city blocks with no fence or guard house. The huge studio building occupied one block; buildings housing film processing and storage occupied another block that was south of the studio. The barracks, with a mess hall and a parking lot behind, it, took up a block just west of the studio. These buildings, belonging to the Army, sat in the midst of multi-story apartment buildings and an assortment of businesses. I was given, for the first time, a bed that was not a bunk in a large bay area. Lockers separated beds from one another, and they weren't placed in long lines.

The whole thing was a wonder. I imagined working on the sound stages across the street, assisting in making training and information films. That bubble burst when I received clarifying orders just days later that assigned me to a "Field Unit" attached to the Pictorial Center. There were two companies connected to the Center. One was a "studio" unit, tied directly to it. Its work supported the production of studio films. The other unit, into which I was placed, went out of the Center on Temporary Duty and focused more on documenting various governmental experiments and testing. I still felt like I had been blessed beyond belief. And I couldn't help but wonder if somehow being recycled in basic and finishing later

than expected hadn't providentially put me in position for this rare assignment.

Only a month later, I received my first temporary duty assignment. I was ordered to travel to Fort Ord, California, to document a Small Arms Weapons Systems (SAWS) Experiment. For five months I recorded squads of men advancing down a firing range, firing either AK 47s or M 16 Rifles. The army was testing the M 16 in its infancy, measuring its performance against the AK 47, the weapon used by the Viet Cong in Vietnam. The goal was to replace the M 14 rifle, presently being used, with the M 16. I walked along with these squads, using my Bell and Howell 16-millimeter motion picture camera to film the firing of these rifles at computerized targets. I also set up remote control cameras along the range facing these shooters so that documentation could be secured from that perspective. In addition, I filmed the firing of other rifles and machine guns. Every few days I would package containers with film I had taken and send them to the Pictorial Center to be processed and distributed for viewing.

I was serving this temporary duty assignment solely for this purpose. The significance of this came into play one day when I was told it was my turn to pull kitchen patrol (KP). This would have involved spending the day peeling potatoes, washing dishes, scrubbing pots and pans, and mopping the floor in the company mess hall. I appealed to the Company Commander and showed him my orders, explaining what I was doing. He immediately dismissed me from having to pull this kind of duty.

Besides accomplishing my mission, there are two things I remember about this duty. It was during this time that I found out that my biological father was being sent to prison for illegal financial dealings. His irresponsible decisions and directionless life had caught up with him. On the one hand I wept for him, but on the other I took delight in his getting what was coming to him. I found myself flushed with embarrassment to bear the Crawford name as I imagined what folks around the Burg must think.

The other thing that marked these five months played into this first thing. It served as a counter to my embarrassment over being a Crawford. My biological father's brother, Jack, and his family lived in Salinas, just a few miles from Fort Ord. Uncle Jack and his family had visited us in the Burg on at least on one occasion. As a Navy pilot he had been stationed in New

BLDG.	NAME	BLDG.	NAME
1	HEADQUARTERS AND MOTION PICTURE STUDIO	23	FILM STORAGE
2	TELEVISION STUDIO	24	BARRACKS WITH MESS HALL
6	FILM DEPOSITORY	S-25	OFFICES AND SUPPLY STOREHOUSE
12	FILM STORAGE	S-26	POST ENGINEER AND PRINTING OFFICES
13	FILM PROCESSING LABORATORY	S-27	POST ENGINEER SHOPS
14	FILM CHEMICAL MIX AND CONTROL	S-28	PROVOST MARSHAL OFFICE

Jersey, close enough to drive to our home. Now he was serving at the Alameda Naval Air Station near San Francisco. He extended a warm welcome and I spent many a Saturday and Sunday hanging out at this Crawford home, spending time with my cousins, being chauffeured by my aunt, Lillian, to touristy places, and playing ping pong with my uncle. Uncle

Jack had the "only retractable Ping Pong table in the world." It could be lifted to the ceiling so that a car could be parked where it sat! My first Christmas away from home wasn't nearly as bad as it could have been because of my uncle and family's hospitality. *

After returning to the Pictorial Center in February of 1966, I received a letter from the Department of the Army commanding me for "your excellent performance of duty during the period September 1965 to 2 February 1966..." It included the following:

"During this period, you carried out your duties of Motion Picture Cameraman with great efficiency, maintaining a high standard of quality in all your work. You displayed a high degree of proficiency in the operation of the 16mm film camera and remote operated gun camera in photo recording each phase of the Small Arm Weapons Systems Experiment. Although you served in the field under conditions which were often uncomfortable and distracting, you continuously maintained your unusually willing and constructive attitude."

The concluding statements made me the proudest.

"Your contribution was an important one to the overall success of the Small Arms Weapons Systems Experiment, in which photographic instrumentation and documentation played an invaluable part. Footage that you obtained was used in the silent briefing series put together immediately at the end of the experiment and will be used in the sound documentary film to be completed in May 1966. By your hard work, initiative, and devotion to duty you reflect great credit on yourself and on your unit."

Addendum: During my months away, I had received my "Secret" Clearance and been promoted to Specialist 4th Class. I had also experienced my second shoulder dislocation while playing ping pong with my Uncle Jack in his garage. A simple roundhouse swipe at the ball with the paddle had resulted in sickening pain and the need for manipulating it back into place.

*Uncle Jack's hospitality has continued to this day. In the fall of 2017, my wife and I traveled to Kirksville, Missouri for four days of enjoyment with him and his wife, Maurine. Then 92 years old, he was spry enough to play two rounds of golf!

Uncle Jack and I in 2017

Fort Huachuca

I spent a little more than a month back at my field photo unit in Long Island City before I received orders for a new assignment to begin on April 2, 1966. I was to serve as an assistant cameraman on a three man crew traveling to Fort Huachuca in southern Arizona to film attack helicopters in flight. This desert base was ideal for this kind of testing. The Cobra and its electronics were our focus. It was being brought online for use in Vietnam and other possible theaters. The production crew included a civilian manager/director, a more experienced Army cameraman named Kurt, and me.

It was not uncommon for a civilian employee of the government to be in charge of film production in our field unit. Sometimes, because of the technical nature of the filming being done, a career film specialist was better suited to fulfill this role. The "studio" unit, directly attached to the Pictorial Center, always included civilians as directors and even cameramen. Large Mitchell Cameras, the same ones used in Hollywood, were used in the training and information films shot on the sound stages. These productions included union gaffers (electricians), grips (logistics) and other stagehands, who were civilians as well.

It turned out that we worked together well, and our twenty days flowed smoothly. Compared to my first assignment at Fort Ord, filming the Small Arms Weapons Systems Experiment, my job was almost too easy--with one exception. Included in my responsibilities was the manning of the clapperboard. The clapperboard was used to indicate the scene and take so that the editors could put the film clips together. This job became quite challenging when we ascended in an old DC-3 with its side door removed so that we could film choppers maneuvering beside us at 8,000 feet.

In order for me to do my job safely, I was given what seemed like a two minute orientation in how to use a parachute. I had to wear one in case I got sucked out of the plane. As a further precaution, I was tethered to the inside of the plane. This was all because I had to position myself as close to the open door as possible, extend my arms out, and hold the clapperboard in front of the camera lens in order to clap the chalkboard while saying what I had written on it, for example, "Scene 1 – Take 1." I prayed that I didn't have to use the parachute, because I had never practiced, and it was very uncomfortable, especially the straps between my legs. Thankfully, all went well during the several days we filmed the Cobras in flight.

We stayed in a motel off base. Our evening meals were taken at local restaurants. I remember enjoying a cocktail or two, eating a juicy steak almost every night, and then puffing on a "good" cigar as a "nightcap." The civilian in charge, whose name escapes me, entertained Kurt and me with stories of his dog. He and his wife lived in New York City and had no children. So their dog WAS their child. He would have us in stitches mimicking "conversations" he had with that little mutt. THAT was the life, at least for 20 days.

We also took some time to explore Tombstone, the legendary western town. It was within easy driving distance of the base. The saloons, hotels, OK Corral, where the Earp brothers and Doc Holiday shot it out with the Clanton Gang, were fascinating. But nothing could top Boot Hill, the cemetery where so many gunslingers were buried.

I flew back to the Pictorial Center repeating those unforgettable words, etched on the most famous Boot Hill wooden marker:

Here Lies

Lester Moore

Four Slugs

From A 44

No Les

No More

Hawaii

I was called into my commanding officer's office in late July 1966. He told me that he wanted me to be in charge of a two-man crew who would travel to Hawaii to document testing that was taking place near Pearl Harbor. He indicated my secret clearance would be needed to ensure security. I remember feeling the blood drain from my face as I considered the responsibility involved. I told him, "I don't think I can do that." He looked at me and said, "Specialist Crawford, we believe you have the leadership and photographic skills to accomplish this mission." He assured me that I would have help making travel arrangements.

So, on August 5, Specialist 4th Class, Dan Hunter, and I (I had been promoted to Specialist 5th Class in June) flew to Hawaii with several hundred pounds of equipment. Over the next couple of days, we settled into our quarters at Hickam Air Force Base, where we would stay for the next four weeks. The unusual part of this was that we were in the Army, staying at an Air Force Base, and on temporary duty to the Navy. We had been given a script of what needed to be filmed. It became clear that this assignment involved the testing of chemical and biological agents. Specifically, our primary responsibility was to spend several days on board a lab ship a hundred miles out of Pearl Harbor, filming the effects of these agents released by aircraft many miles downwind.

The weather out at sea was not cooperative for the first two weeks. Because of storms, the sea was too rough to accomplish our task. So, Dan and I filmed what we needed to on land. We spent time at Barbers Point Naval Air Station shooting a fighter jet taking off and other important scenes for the script. But for most of this two-week period, we enjoyed the sun and sunbathing women at Waikiki Beach. We lived the life of beach bums, eating in nice restaurants and checking out the bar and dance scene. In fact, I met a stunning "California Girl" who was on vacation from Los Angeles. I think she was more curious than really interested in a G.I., and so that connection went nowhere fast.

Well, the sea finally calmed, and we traveled out to our destination in the Pacific on the ship that was to be our "set" for a week. Once we were about 100 miles out, the ship was buttoned up, and we experienced the life of a sailor, entertaining ourselves the best we could, eating and socializing in the mess hall, and sleeping in those stacked steel-framed bunk beds. After the bacterial agent had passed over the ship we were allowed to emerge, and our filming of its effects on materials in Petri dishes and plants began. Once we had gotten the footage we needed, we were provided transport back to Pearl Harbor. A large tug boat, ballasted for sea duty, pulled up beside the ship, and we transferred ourselves and equipment to it.

During the transfer, I experienced shoulder trauma for the third time. The tug was rolling, even though tethered to the lab ship. As I stepped from a gangway to the tug, I had to grab a pipe to steady myself. In doing this, my shoulder dislocated, and once again experiencing pain that almost made me sick, I had to manipulate it back into the socket. It was then that I determined, upon returning to New York and the Pictorial Center, to seek medical attention to get this fixed.

On the way into Pearl Harbor, the captain of the tug decided that we would do some swimming in the middle of the ocean. The experience of diving off a ship with no land in sight was unforgettable. I can say that I spent very little time in the water for fear of attracting sharks, and that I avoided razor sharp barnacles by catching the tug's ladder when it rolled down towards me. The return trip to New York was uneventful. Another growth point had been achieved, having been entrusted with such a large responsibility. It was good that I had no idea of what awaited me at "home" in New York City.

Limited Duty

When I returned from the thirty day assignment in Hawaii, I discovered that I had received special orders. I was assigned to a signal unit whose destination was "somewhere in Southeast Asia." I knew this meant I was being sent to Vietnam as a combat photographer. Since I had determined to do something about my shoulder upon returning to the Pictorial Center, I immediately made arrangements to see an Orthopedic Surgeon at St. Albans Naval Hospital in Brooklyn.

He examined my shoulder and had x-rays taken. A second consultation resulted in the diagnosis that I had a severe dislocation issue that would require surgery. He also said, "this will remove you from those orders."

To say I was relieved is an understatement. I did not want to be in the field, in a combat situation, having to jump several feet from a hovering chopper, with a shoulder that could dislocate, incapacitating me. So, I was scheduled for surgery in the late fall of 1966 at St. Albans. Dr. Parks, the Navy doctor who had diagnosed my problem, fixed my shoulder. I spent the next three months at the hospital, first in recovery and then in rehabilitation. The pain at first was excruciating. I spent a week of unforgettable discomfort, only able to sleep on my back. My right arm was first in a cast to keep it stable. After a month, I was able to have the cast removed and was in a sling for a month and a half.

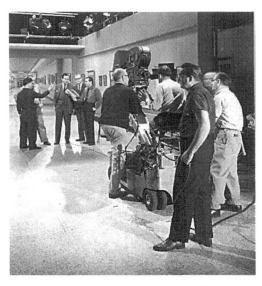

Returning to the Pictorial Center in February 1967, I was placed on light or limited duty. Due to complete my three year enlistment in November of that year, I remained in that status until I was separated from active duty. Since I could no longer travel, I was placed in a still photography lab where I helped with processing and printing film. I became proficient at producing "Set Stills"--pictures taken on sound stages to document motion picture filming being done. I also processed and printed film taken by crews on temporary duty assignments, including Viet Nam. I got close to the other soldiers working in the lab, and on my 22nd birthday they threw me quite a party.

Thinking of people with whom I became friends, three guys come to mind. Larry Adams was my roommate. After my promotion to Specialist 4th Class, I earned the right to live in a room. Prior to being drafted, Larry had been a lifeguard on

Daytona Beach. He was resentful of being plucked from this beach boy lifestyle. He knew Uncle Sam owned him for two years and that he could be sent anywhere. Larry and I spent many a Saturday or Sunday enjoying Central Park and checking out various bars and restaurants in Manhattan. I will never forget Larry's reaction when a dust ball was found under his bed during one of the "white glove" weekly inspections. He stood during our general assembly and barely containing his anger, his voice shaking, said, "I don't know how that dust ball got there, but it must have been an act of God!" We laughed about it later.

Benny McGee was a Georgia boy. He was from Thomaston and had been married briefly. He wore glasses with small circular lenses and had this smile that betrayed a condescending attitude. Compared with many of us, Benny was a man of experience, a regular Don Juan. He fascinated me with his tale of experiencing a temporary assignment in Vietnam. And he delighted in describing his sexploits. I wasn't sure how much to believe at times, but there was something about him which I found likable.

Then there was the square-jawed West Virginian. I don't remember his name, but we hung out mostly in the NCO (Non-Commissioned Officers) Club. The NCO Club was a bar in the basement of the barracks. It offered cheap drinks, music and an opportunity to swap yarns and make up stuff. The West Virginian would entertain me with his stories from the hills and hollers. He introduced me to the descriptive phrase, "Pine Jumpas." This was a colloquial reference to country bumpkins. I think he was intimating that these people were idiots who thought they could leap over pine trees. His disregard for most people and irreverence for life in general were reflected in his favorite saying: "F'em all, big and small, all but six--leave them for pallbearers." I sometimes wonder what happened to him and those other memorable characters.

My 22nd Birthday

Manhattan, Moondog and Mystery

During my time at the Army Pictorial Center, the Borough of Manhattan in New York City became my place of escape. The three subway stops it took me to travel there from Astoria in Long Island City in Queens became almost as familiar as Water Street into the Burg. The scenery along the route was never changing and arrival time and place predictable. The difference was that the "wheels" I used involved clicking and clacking my way along with an intriguing group of fellow travelers who generally kept to themselves. It was as though I was the only passenger on the train most of the time.

Central Park, in the heart of Manhattan, was a place where I spent a great deal of time. Many a Saturday or Sunday it would be teeming with people out to relax on the lawns near Central Park Lake or the Reservoir. Many a couple or group could be seen lounging on blankets, enjoying a glass of wine and conversation. The laughter of children playing games or flying kites helps form the mural I still have in my mind of those days in the park. There was always the presence of mounted police, reminding everyone that law and order would be kept amidst such a crowd. In fact, the horses were magnets for young and old. It was not uncommon to see people gathered around the officers chatting with them while petting their mount. It provided a treasure trove of scenes for picture taking. Although I limited my park walking at night-- even then it could be dangerous--I did attend two concerts there. It made a great venue for popular rock groups. The

Animals or Lovin' Spoonful would have never appeared in the Burg, or even Jamestown.

Landmarks like the Empire State Building and the RCA Building were special places where I could enjoy a panoramic view of the city. A sweet and pretty woman whom I had met in Jamestown while on leave spent time with me in Manhattan seeing the sights. Gunn was on her way back to Sweden, where she had her permanent home. She surprised me when she spit off the top of the Empire State Building on a beautiful sun-drenched day. A highlight was taking the subway to Battery Park so that we could ride the Staten Island Ferry. We also got tickets to an off-Broadway musical and enjoyed delightful hours in the theater. I bid her bon voyage as she boarded the ship docked in the Hudson River. Although we corresponded for a period of time, I never saw her again.

There was a bar/restaurant on the Upper East Side where I loved to relax. The main attraction for me at Brandy's was the singer songwriter, Bobby Hebb. He was a frequent performer and always included the song, "Sunny," in his repertoire. He had written that song, which would rise to the top of music charts, during one of his many appearances at Brandy's. Some said that the song was birthed out of tragic deaths of his brother and President Kennedy. But Bobby always maintained that it was inspired by a relationship and the particular night sky when he wrote it.

Another attraction for me was a character named Moondog. I referred to him as "The Blind Viking." I always encountered him at the same spot, the corner of 53rd Street and 6th Avenue. He had long hair and a bushy beard and wore a horned Viking helmet. He stood with a spear in one hand and wore a long cloak. Around his neck were two leather strings, one holding a hollowed-out cow's hoof and the other a leather sheath. The leather sheath held poetry that he had written. Many times, I came back to the base with a piece of his poetry for which I had paid a dime. The cow's hoof was the money receptacle. Moondog was such an intriguing figure, standing with that blind stare and silent most of the time. In my encounters with him, I managed to engage him in limited conversation. I asked him about his poetry and music writing, his background and his philosophy. He told me he had been blinded when he was sixteen years old in a farm accident. For the most part he was self-educated and was a street musician when not appearing as "the Viking of 6th Avenue." His name was Louis Thomas Hardin, and he had given himself the name "Moondog" in honor of a dog who howled at the moon. Also, he had a great interest in Nordic mythology and kept an altar to Thor, the god of thunder.

All of these experiences and people were threads in a colorful tapestry that was being woven in my life. I didn't see it at the time, but God had me in His hands. The really mysterious part of this time in the Army occurred when I had two dreams in which I felt deeply that I was being called to be a pastor! How could this be? I was making the best of my life without any spiritual focus. I hadn't darkened the door of a church, with one exception, in years. The exception was when I snuck into a Lutheran Cathedral in Manhattan one night and had a weird monologue with God about the void in my life. I wasn't seriously seeking to reconnect with God and yet He wanted me to be a... pastor?? A hernia, discovered during my separation physical, kept me in the Army for nineteen days beyond the day I was to be discharged from active duty. A chaplain, who stopped by to check on me after surgery at St. Albans Naval Hospital, provided me with a sounding board

for my strange dreams. He simply shrugged his shoulders, not knowing what to say.

And so, the weaving continued, full of mystery and wonder, until I would receive further providential light following my days in the military. On December 1, 1967, I headed home to Bemus Point, after belonging to Uncle Sam for three years and nineteen days.

Home

Cross on the shore of Findley Lake, where my Baptism was

affirmed. This is where I heard God's voice through Dr. Kinlaw. We

have attended this Bible camp for the past 42 years.

FREE!

I arrived home on December 1, 1967 with a separation check for $464.72, a heart filled with life-changing memories, and a duffle bag bulging with my belongings-- some civilian clothes, combat boots, shoes, fatigues, a dress uniform, and hats. Although I had much for which to be grateful, words cannot describe the joy I felt to no longer belong to Uncle Sam. Mom and Dad welcomed me into their home on Harold Avenue in Bemus Point. I still had a bed, and I could once again enjoy my mom's exceptional baking and cooking. The only thing I didn't want was the chicken. I needed a break from the favorite meat of the U.S. Army, so it seemed. One of my first purchases was a 1960 Buick Electra, since dad had had to junk my Lincoln, whose trunk floor had fallen onto the driveway.

It didn't take long to discover that things had changed. Or, to put it more accurately, I had changed. I was no longer the immature young man who had left home seeking direction. I was now a veteran who bore scars, literal and figurative, and who had successfully navigated the expectations of something much bigger than I. I had been given and fulfilled some significant responsibilities and built a confidence lacking prior to enlisting. In short, I had become an adult and established my own identity. My parents had their own routines and expectations of those who lived in their house, for good reason. My sisters and brother were still their responsibility. I didn't fit.

About a month later I had found an apartment on North Main Street in Jamestown. I was about to begin studies at Jamestown Community College (JCC), and it was a quick drive to the campus. This was to be the first of two apartments I rented in completing a year and a half at the college. I found a job at a Quality Markets Grocery Store in the city. I was once again a part-time stock boy, the manager flexing my hours to fit with my classes. Mom helped me with setting up housekeeping and provided me with some recipes so that I wouldn't "starve." I took delight in making my first meatloaf.

It was a bit lonely at times, but I was only a few miles from Bemus Point, and I got busy with college and work. I will never forget the visit I had from two men dressed in suits--government investigators--who quizzed me about the information I might have divulged regarding the work I had done in Hawaii when we filmed the chemical–biological testing. Thankfully they believed me when I insisted that I had told no one about this classified assignment.

My freshman year in college began with a vague goal of becoming a social worker, and the realization that I was going to need to carry a dictionary in my briefcase at all times. A few classes with other veterans and high school graduates, and the reading assignments we were given, made me aware of how vocabulary and spelling-poor I was. I say "other veterans" because many of us were there taking advantage of the G.I. Bill. Most of my basic college expenses (tuition and books) were paid for with this money. And unlike some of my fellow vets, who wasted time playing cards in the commons, I was serious about getting an education.

But I needed additional income in order to live on my own and was thankful for my job at Quality Markets. It was located on the east side of Jamestown and was ideal for walk-up traffic. The manager, who had the nickname, "Whiz" or "Whizzer," was a no-nonsense boss who expected employees to be on time, to work hard, and to keep the break-room tidy. His favorite saying was, "DO something, even if it is wrong!" He had a sense of humor, but it was rarely seen. I remember not being able to find a tie I had left on a hook in the break room so that I could wear it the next time I came into work (stock boys wore ties during store hours). It was nowhere to be found. I discovered that the Whizzer, in one of his "clean sweeps" around the store, thought this dangling piece of material was an eyesore and needed "shit canning!" This job, full of competitions to see who could bag groceries the fastest and typical stock room shenanigans, helped get me through that first phase of living on my own as a college student.

Settled but Unsettled

I was settling into the routines of my exciting new freedom. I was in a Liberal Arts curriculum, which meant I was taking basic courses in a variety of subjects that would help me have a good educational foundation for whatever I decided to do with my life. Since I had a notion of becoming a social worker, I plunged into a course in Sociology, as well as courses in Psychology, Philosophy, and English and History. I had decided that my vocational direction would NOT involve the need to take math and science courses!

I found attending Community College an enjoyable challenge. Part of this was the realization that I was so far behind in my ability to write and even speak articulately, that I needed to spend extra time reading and expanding my use of the English language. That dictionary that I carried in my briefcase became indispensable.

My work at the grocery store became a welcome relief from the hours spent in my apartment or in the library studying. I also found time to renew my acquaintance with bars in Bemus Point and in the area near the college. I looked forward to seeing old friends like the Bemus Boys and some classmates from high school. I also pursued some of my still photography interests from the Army. I would often take my Pentax Spotmatic Camera with me and walk around Jamestown to see what, and who, I could capture on film. Rainy nights became my friend.

But I was unsettled. The sense that something was missing gnawed at my soul. The times themselves were unsettling. Abby Hoffman wanted to destroy all laws, even the law of gravity. The Vietnam War was becoming even more distasteful, and veterans returning home were disrespected. I had to deal with smartass young professors who took every opportunity to criticize the government and military. My history professor would sit cross-legged on his desk, spinning his twisted-arm-chair-take on the morality of our involvement. Racial upheaval was occurring as the Black Panthers engaged in violence, while Martin Luther King Jr. was shaking the foundations with his peaceful revolution. And there were those two dreams I had experienced while still in the Army. These dreams would play an even larger role than I thought as this part of my life unfolded.

In February of that winter semester I noticed an advertisement on a bulletin board in the commons area. It announced a presentation to take place at a small church just off campus. The focus was on what Christianity had to say about the decline of morality in our culture. Since I felt somewhat adrift and unfulfilled, in some undeniable internal way, I decided to attend. It was there, for the first time in a long time, that I encountered what I believed to be a sound perspective on how to navigate the disturbing currents of our culture, as well as how to approach my own malaise. Spiritual/Biblical absolutes were lifted up in the midst of overwhelming relativism. That experience motivated me to darken the door of the church my sister and I had attended during our year living in Jamestown after mom and dad had been married.

I mentioned in the section, "Life around the Burg," that I had come to faith while attending the Evangelical United Brethren Church in Frewsburg. After moving to Jamestown just before my senior year in high school, my sister, Connie, and I, had transferred our membership to Kidder Memorial EUB Church. It was within walking distance of our apartment on Barker Street. The first Sunday in March 1968, I found myself sitting in a pew for the first time since sometime in 1963, listening to a Biblical sermon. The preacher, Rev. H. Ray Harris, announced during the worship service that in the latter part of the month, a series of spiritual renewal services would be held, led by a missionary friend by the name of Jack Marshall. I heard this announcement for the next two Sundays and decided to hear what Marshall had to say.

I can best describe what followed as finding my Spiritual Home.

Welcomed Home!

Rev. Jack Marshall, the featured preacher for the renewal services, and his wife, Jerri, were serving as missionaries in Japan. Home on furlough, he had agreed to preach each evening, beginning on Monday and culminating in the Sunday morning service at the end of the week.

Feeling spiritually adrift and sensing a void in my life, I decided to hear what Rev. Marshall had to say. I don't remember the content of his sermons, but I know I resonated with the Biblical texts he used, and how they related to my life. I was drawn back to multiple evening services. I felt that something deep inside me was being stirred – the Lord of Life was addressing longings that had remained unfulfilled, through even my best efforts. At the end of each message there was an invitation to come forward, kneel at an altar, and commit to following Jesus Christ. I held out.

During the morning service, on Sunday, March 24th, Marshall gave a particularly impassioned invitation, following a powerfully incisive sermon. I had been unalterably convicted of my need to turn my life over to someone who could satisfy all my longings and replace me as the caption of my ship. I kept hesitating. As time ticked away, I was overwhelmed with the sense that it might be "now or never." I slowly stood up where I was sitting and moved down the aisle of the sanctuary of Kidder Church to the altar rail. Kneeling there, I surrendered, knowing that along with this, was my response to those two mysterious dreams I had had in the Army. I committed myself to becoming a pastor, however that was to unfold.

Kneeling at the rail I became aware of two women who had apparently followed and knelt on each side of me. Elinor Hare and Rosy Lesch had worked with youth when my sister, Connie, and I had been involved with the church during the year that we lived nearby. Years later, here they were, lovingly supporting me as I made the biggest commitment of my life. They became two of my most ardent cheerleaders as I arrived Home, at the Father's House, and launched into my new life as a disciple of the Lord Jesus Christ. Also, in the congregation that morning was Lee Ailing, who had been my Cub Scout Den Mother in 1954 – 1956, when we lived in the Projects on Forrest Avenue before moving to the Burg.

The Harrises invited me to their home following the service that morning. I discovered a home, full of "the milk of human kindness," a phrase Amanda Harris would use many times over the ensuing years. I was treated to hospitality, including a delicious meal and warm fellowship. Jack, who the Lord had used in a life-changing way in my life, and his wife, Jerri, extended an intensely personal embrace, and the Harrises became my mentors and second family. They "took pity" on this young man, twenty-two years old, who they knew would need all the spiritual and material encouragement and support they could give. I became the son they never had.

... So, he got up and went to his father. But while he was still a long way off, the father saw him and was filled with compassion for him; He ran to his son, threw his arms around him and kissed him.

Luke 15:20   "The Prodigal Son"

Photos: Jack and Jerri Marshall;
Amanda and H. Ray Harris

A New Identity

I often refer to surrendering myself to the Lord on March 24, 1968, as my "mature commitment." I never want to discount the "coming to faith" I experienced as a teenager in the Burg. I glimpsed the grip God had on my life. It's just that I drifted away, having no real spiritual mooring. In effect, I had attempted to captain my own ship--run my own life. And I discovered that I couldn't do a very good job. Surrendering to Christ and his call to be a pastor meant that I needed to establish a new identity. How was that going to happen?

Well, to begin with, my pastor and his wife, H. Ray and Amanda Harris, took me under their wing. As I mentioned previously, I became the son they didn't have. They had a daughter, Helene, who was their only child. She lived with her family near Harrisburg, PA. The Harrises became "Mom" and "Pop." I was invited to make their home my home. Now, my mom and dad's home was mine as well--I just couldn't live there. I still lived in my apartment, but whenever I needed a delicious home-cooked meal, seasoned with spiritual counsel, I could just stop by. I needed a great deal of spiritual direction. I had stepped out of a morally undisciplined life, particularly when it came to "wine and women... and language." My priorities began to change from that "Surrender Sunday" on. I was like a sponge, absorbing the shaping I received through Mom and Pop Harris.

I experienced first-hand a pastor's workshop, as well as a parsonage full of hospitality. I never remember Pop preaching a sermon that didn't reflect thorough preparation. Hours in his study, meditating on Scripture, consulting commentaries and praying, resulted in the most helpful homilies. And he was quick to offer correction to me if he heard, or observed, my old worldly habits still putting the "squeeze" on my life. Mom exuded compassion. She was always prepared to "throw another chicken in the pot," if she saw a person or family who could use a good meal. And she worked with youth in the church, even though she was in her sixties! In fact, she encouraged me to join her in leading the Senior High Sunday School Class at Kidder. She exemplified loving people into God's Kingdom in every way she could. I felt completely welcomed into their lives and home.

Not only did I have a new family, but I also discovered a Christian community at the Community College. I joined Intervarsity Christian Fellowship, a group of students who sought to encourage one another in dealing with a milieu that elevated free thinking as well as free love. It was a culture I knew I had to separate myself from if I was to learn the ways of a disciple. And it was a culture that desperately needed to hear about, and experience, the love of God in Jesus Christ. Our small group of fellow believers provided support and strength for making a difference spiritually.

With such a supportive family and community, I was determined to live differently. And like so many new converts, I am sure that I said and did some dumb things in my clumsy attempt to be faithful to my new identity. But I forged on and somehow my professors became aware of this identity. Mr. Eckstrand, my philosophy teacher, grew fond of asking me to share the Christian perspective when we dealt with moral problems.

In fact, it was a bit frustrating, because I considered myself a babe in the faith, far from the resident expert in spiritual matters. But I would give the most reasoned response I could muster, and he would receive it in a most appreciative way. On the other hand, my Sociology professor expressed much disdain for Christianity. I think he delighted in putting me in my place, as he spun out his well-prepared lectures on the critical importance of sociological research and influence. Something led him to exclaim one day in class, "If God came down beside me and said, 'Hi, I'm God,' I would commit myself to a mental institution!" I remember him casting a smirking glance in my direction.

The firmness of my commitment to Christ, and the loving

support of a Christian family and community, only strengthened my resolve to grow in my understanding of what it meant to be a witness in skeptical and even hostile territory. Surely higher education was just that. I cherished my new identity.

Early Markings

Coming to Christ in a mature way on March 24, 1968, was the beginning of a radical new way of life. Being surrounded by a host of cheerleaders, who were also eager to offer instruction, was critical. I was truly a newborn baby dependent upon those much more mature in the faith. But I also quickly came to the realization that through some stumbling, it was up to me to establish a pattern of behavior reflective of my commitment to be a disciple, the Spirit of God being my helper.

Alone in my apartment, I remember more than once experiencing uncertainty as to the reality of what had happened to me. I challenged God to prove his presence by doing this or that. These were trivial things that have long since fallen into the depths of the forgotten, but to this day, the silliness of this strikes me, along with the thought that God proved faithful even in these infantile moments. This included my first very self-conscious attempts at conversation with God. Prayer was something that I knew needed to permeate my daily routines. I began to learn that God cared about even the minor and sometimes annoying things.

Offering table grace became a priority, even in public. I would often catch breakfast in a restaurant before attending classes at JCC. I didn't like to eat alone in my apartment. One morning, after ordering bacon and eggs, I bowed my head to offer thanks for the sacrifice of the pig, who had given much more than the chicken. When I looked up, the cook, who had prepared my eggs and bacon on the grill behind the counter where I was sitting, asked me "What's wrong with it?" I quickly assured him that my looking down was not a form of disgust but that I was offering thanks!

I spent enough time in the college library that one of the librarians got to know me. One day I went to the desk and asked to check out the musical, "Hair." I had heard some of the music on the radio and wanted to find out more about it. The librarian gave me the album and added, "I thought you were a Christian?" I knew that some of the lyrics I had listened to didn't exactly reflect the values to which I was now being exposed, but I liked the music anyway. It didn't take me long, however, to discover that the whole musical was a glorification of the Hippie counterculture and promoted the sexual "revolution." Apparently, the stage production included nudity, profanity, the illegal use of drugs and disrespect for the American Flag.

As I "chalked" out my new life and identity, another "marking" involved dating. This was an area that needed serious change. Previously, there was one goal in getting to know a woman-- physical intimacy. I began to understand that as a Christian, this "goal" was reserved for marriage. The focus now was in valuing a woman for who she was and not for what I could get. In a larger way, I worked on valuing people as Christ did, loving them rather than using them. The selfishness with which I had approached relationships became apparent. An important piece of this was looking for someone who shared these same values.

During these early days, which included my year and a half at the Community College, I dated women who were not only committed to Jesus Christ, but they were iron-clad in their determination to be pure, to not use or be used. This was hard for me, but I was experiencing the Lord's School of

Discipleship. This involved shedding the self-centered values and behavior patterns I had developed over the years and becoming the man God was calling and shaping me to be. I sought to become a God-shaped man; a man who had his priorities right in caring for God and others.

Intervarsity Christian Fellowship

I previously mentioned a Christian support group I discovered at JCC. Intervarsity Christian Fellowship was a campus-recognized organization that met weekly, using a college classroom. An adjunct faculty member who was a part of the nursing program served as our adviser. There were about twenty students who considered themselves members, most of whom showed up for our weekly meetings. The ratio of women to men was something like five to one. While some within the group found dating partners, our focus was on having fun as Christians, encouraging one another, and equipping each other for providing some sort of witness to our college community.

We tried to have a discussion topic for our meetings that involved the Bible and a book or guide produced by Intervarsity Press. These publications became a source of understanding faith and how it could impact the culture. I appreciated the fact that there were Christian scholars and pastors who provided tools for strengthening our faith, as well as engaging skeptics and unbelievers. Writers like John R.W. Stott and Francis Shaeffer became my companions.

We also had monthly outings for fun, and we sometimes attended church services together. I established life-long friendships during the almost year and a half I was a part of this group. Bill Flynn, from Indiana, was a veteran like me. He had served for four years in the Navy. We immediately discovered that we had a similar sense of humor, as well as a like passion for following Christ. Bill had been a believer since boyhood, and so I had someone whose more mature faith served as a model. He went on to Purdue University, where he received a degree in engineering. Our friendship continued through the years and my wife, Bev, and I have visited Bill and his wife, Linda, several times wherever they lived.

Alba Cruz became a friend during that time. We both furthered our education at Houghton College, and Alba invited me to participate in her wedding when she married Doug Arters. We have touched base over the ensuing years and plan on getting together in the near future.

Several of us who were involved with Intervarsity Christian Fellowship on the campus of Jamestown Community College made decisions to attend Houghton College, a small Christian Liberal Arts College, 85 miles east of Jamestown. Our connection with JCC and Intervarsity influenced our attending Urbana 1970, a major student mission conference sponsored by Intervarsity Christian Fellowship and held on the campus of the University of Illinois at Urbana--Champaign. I will never forget traveling there through the snows of December, and then being inspired by the

BILL AND LINDA FLYNN

Biblical teaching of John Stott, and other noted Christian leaders.

For me, the decision to attend Houghton College was easy. I knew I needed to work on a degree that would prepare me for seminary and pastoral ministry. I had first discovered Houghton through traveling there with mom and pop Harris. They knew a young man who was a ministerial student there and I was introduced to the campus. I was impressed, and had no problem transferring enough coursework after a year and a half to begin as a sophomore.

It was time to launch out from the safe harbor of nurture I had experienced through family and friends and begin to navigate the rapids of maturation on my own.

"PLAYFULL BILL"

Pleasant Valley

As my excitement grew, anticipating my move to Houghton, I was offered the opportunity to serve as interim pastor of a small country church in the middle of Chautauqua County. It was a three-month summer appointment that would fill the gap between the end of the semester at JCC and the beginning of my Houghton College experience. The Rev. Don Modisher, the Superintendent of the Jamestown District of the Western New York Conference of the United Methodist Church, had called me and asked me if I would be willing to assume this responsibility. I had found myself in the United Methodist Church, following the merger the year before of my denomination, the Evangelical United Brethren Church, with the Methodist denomination. Pop Harris had let Rev. Modisher know that I was going to be preparing for pastoral ministry, and he in turn saw this as a good way for me to gain some experience.

So as of June 1, 1969, I became the pastor of the Pleasant Valley United Methodist Church. Sunday worship consisted of between 15 and 20 folks, spanning the age spectrum, who met in a one-room church building. One extended family made up most of the congregation. A woman named Esther was the Matriarch of the church. She was in her 70's and had been a member of the congregation for decades. She made many of the decisions regarding everything from leadership to building upkeep to expenditure of funds. Far from being dictatorial, Esther was one of the sweetest, most devout, and

supportive people I encountered in all of pastoral ministry. In fact, for the rest of her life, she would send me notes, letting me know how she was doing and what was happening in Pleasant Valley.

Having such a person in the congregation made my life as a complete novice much easier. Of course, I also had the wise counsel of Pop Harris, who gave me pointers for sermon preparation and guided me in conducting my first funeral service. Mom Harris came out on more than one occasion and played the piano, particularly when I broke out my cornet for special music and hymn accompaniment.

Since I was not credentialed, only employed by the District Superintendent, I was not qualified to serve communion or to officiate at weddings. During a Jamestown District meeting for new pastors in July, I was introduced to John Cooke.

John had recently graduated from Asbury Seminary in Wilmore, Kentucky, and had been appointed to the Ashville-Blockville Charge. He offered to come to Pleasant Valley and serve communion. The bond that John and I formed has lasted over the years. He was one of the people who influenced me in my decision to attend Asbury Seminary.

Pleasant Valley was my initiation into what would be a forty-year experience of pastoral ministry in the United Methodist Church, and I am forever grateful for this first opportunity to be able to serve and be surrounded by such beautiful, unique and precious people.

The Keith House

My room at the top of the stairs

In early September 1969, after saying "goodbye" to my little church family at Pleasant Valley, I packed up my 1960 Buick Electra and headed for Houghton. When I had made the arrangements for college housing, the idea of staying in a dorm with a bunch of younger guys had little appeal. I had spent three years in the army and a year and a half living by myself. There weren't a lot of options, since Houghton was a very small "island" in what seemed like the middle of nowhere. A place named Wellsville was the largest town nearby. It had a population of about 7,000 and was located almost thirty miles south towards the Pennsylvania line. Housing, other than in a dormitory on campus, was limited. However, I found the ideal place! The Keith family lived on Rt. 19, the major highway through Houghton. Buddy Keith was both a teacher and an administrator at Houghton Academy, a small Christian school located in Houghton. His wife, Lenora, was a homemaker and mom to four children. To supplement Buddy's income, they rented a room and a small apartment to Houghton College students. The timing was right, and the room was available. Their home became my home for the next three years.

The room was in their home, at the top of a stairway, on the second floor. I had to walk through the front door, past the dining room, and up the stairs to access my room. The Keith children, John, Ellen, Tim and Miriam also had rooms on that floor. We all shared a bathroom on the first floor. It was a wonderful home, full of warmth and laughter. It made the transition from larger and more familiar settings much easier. I had a desk and some shelving for my growing book collection. With a fairly quiet house, considering I was living with a family of six, I was able to accomplish an amazing amount of class work preparation. On occasion, I was invited to join the family for a meal or watch Buffalo Bills football on the TV in the basement. Buddy and Lenora were good Wesleyan folks who lived out their Christian faith.

The Keith House was located across from the only restaurant in town, the Houghton Inn. The Inn offered a limited menu, and I ate there occasionally, mostly taking my meals in the dining room of East Hall, a dormitory on the campus. Four miles east of Houghton was Fillmore, where I did my laundry at a Laundromat. I was able to park my car just a short distance from where I roomed. I walked back and forth to the campus, located on a plateau and focused around a quad. It was calming living in a community where twelve hundred students, one hundred faculty and staff and townspeople, for the most part, shared the same ultimate focus--honoring Jesus Christ. Even the one barber attended the only house of worship in town, the Houghton Wesleyan Church. And it was not surprising when Ted initiated a conversation about faith. There were two or three business owners who didn't fit the "mold," who were more "worldly," but who supplied needed services, and who were respected by the community. Frankly, I found these people refreshing.

While it was healthy for me to live in this unique setting while the Lord shaped me as a disciple and as I prepared for ministry as a pastor, the almost seamless sameness would become something from which I sought relief at times. Driving to Wellsville for a "gut buster" at Texas Hots, or to Jamestown for the weekend, worked very well.

Buddy and Lenora Keith

Building a Foundation

I went to Houghton College because I understood that it would provide me with a good foundation for fulfilling my calling to be a pastor. I liked the fact that it was a small college connected with the Wesleyan Church, a sister denomination to mine. I had, by default, become a United Methodist because of the merger in 1968. I was comfortable with what I understood about Methodism and its roots in the Wesley tradition. The college and my denomination were in the same theological stream. Another appeal was that Houghton College was a small school. I felt I wouldn't be overwhelmed by what could be the impersonal setting of a large college or university.

Since the United Methodist Church required seminary in order to be an ordained Elder, I needed to do the preparatory work to pursue an advanced degree, called a Master of Divinity. And since I had limited involvement in a local church, I had to make up for a lack of Biblical knowledge and theological understanding. In consultation with the guidance office, I decided that a Bachelor of Arts in Religion would provide me with a good foundation. The curriculum necessary to complete this degree included courses to equip pastors, like preaching, Bible study, theology, the Greek language and Christian Ethics.

I most eagerly plunged into these classes, knowing that they would prepare me ultimately for what I would be doing for my vocational life. I found that over-all my professors reflected a depth of expertise that stimulated my passion to learn as much as I could. Three of these teachers stand out as to influencing my life, as well as equipping me for the next level of my preparation for pastoral ministry.

Irv Reist was my theology professor. He was a relatively young man who amazed me by the depth of his knowledge, covering the spectrum of 20th Century theological thinking. He had read the massive Church Dogmatics, by Karl Barth and could converse knowledgeably about evangelical theologians such as Carl F.H. Henry and liberals like Paul Tillich. Professor Reist had a mesmerizing combination of intensity and informality that made learning a joy. On occasion, he would invite students to his home near Fillmore and have class around a big oak table, his wife serving us homemade pastry with our coffee. He delighted in sharing unforgettable tidbits about the lives of theologians. One I will always remember was when he told us about the Swiss Theologian, Karl Barth. Barth was on a tour of the United States in 1962 and was asked by a student in Chicago if he could sum up his whole life's work in one sentence. He said it could be summed up in something he learned at his mother's knee as a boy. It was this: "Jesus loves me this I know, for the Bible tells me so." Theological studies became such an interest that I completed an Independent Study in the theology of Paul Tillich with Mr. Reist. The theological foundation that was built during these days gave me confidence as I looked forward to seminary and then pastoral ministry in a diverse church.

Dr. Carl Schultz taught Old Testament Studies and was most responsible for initially spurring my interest in this area of the Bible. He was always thoroughly prepared and made the Old Testament come alive. There was never an attempt to explain away the supernatural power of God displayed in the history of Israel. In fact, Professor Schultz helped us to understand how God worked through redemptive history to bring about salvation and the fulfillment of his covenants. He had an engaging way of encouraging dialogue and never put down curiosity or thinking outside the box. He was always approachable and in a one-on-one encounter, I knew his attention was riveted on my concern. The Old Testament, as a focus for seminary, and in my preaching, can be traced back to Dr. Shultz. Interestingly, during the time I served as a District Superintendent (1991 – 1995), he was a pastor on my district. He did this in his "spare time," believing that it helped him as a teacher in preparing men and women for pastoral ministry. He was always gracious and kidded me about being "his boss."

Finally, I think I had Warren Woolsey for courses that covered the whole New Testament, except for the Book of Revelation. I came to realize quickly that he had a scintillating way of getting students to engage the New Testament and understand how important it was for shaping our lives. I hung on almost every word out of his mouth during his lectures. There was hardly a semester that I didn't have him as a teacher during my three years at Houghton. Even murky texts came alive as he dissected Greek words and syntax. Although he was approachable, he had a way of seeming to emerge out of his scholarly study closet, captivate us for a while with his findings, and then disappear.

I found him a bit intimidating, but I remember two life-shaping encounters I had with him outside the classroom. On one occasion, I met him in the hallway of the building where he taught his classes, after I had been late with a research paper. I apologized to him, and he must have sensed that I was unnecessarily beating myself up with the guilt I felt (something with which I had an ongoing battle). He listened intently to what I said, and then responded, "Well, don't wear a hair shirt." In other words, don't be like someone in the middle ages, who put on a shirt made of course hair, in order to assuage guilt and "pay" for their failure to do what they should.

The other encounter I had with Mr. Woolsey happened one day outside the campus library. I met him on the sidewalk and told him about a new spiritual insight I had about shedding anything that could be an impediment to my relationship with the Lord. Again, he listened intently, and said, "Be careful, you know 'well, there goes my bowling ball out the window.'" He was challenging a notion he was hearing that I had to practice extreme self-denial and stop doing anything that was fun in my zealousness to please God. It amounted to a course re-direction on my journey towards maturity in Christ.

I ended up with a fist full of notes for each course I took from Mr. Woolsey. For the first few years of pastoral ministry I often consulted these during sermon preparation. And there were times when preaching that I felt like I had said something just the way he would say it. It gave me a profoundly good feeling.

Extracurricular

M any of us who were students at Houghton College referred to Houghton as "the island." The elevation of the campus, located on a plateau near the Genesee River, contributed to this, but the main reason for this description was its atypical homogenous culture. It was an evangelical Christian community in a rural setting dotted with hamlets, villages, and small cities, which were typically diverse in spirituality. This "island" offered what I needed in

my early journey towards maturity in the faith. I could be immersed in a Christian culture that was, in a sense, separate from the distractions and temptations of the world around it. It was a beautiful place to be. I was there mainly so that I could be equipped academically to deal with seminary and pastoral ministry, but, of course, I involved myself with many extracurricular activities. I was not cut out to spend my life in the classroom or library.

On campus there were a variety of opportunities for these activities. I played some basketball in the little band-box campus gym. Sometimes faculty and students combined to form teams. I dusted off my cornet and took lessons from one of our music professors. He cracked me up with the metaphors and images he used to try to get me to "play right." Honestly, sometimes I would break into laughter when he was trying to be serious about technique. It didn't go over very well, and my more formal training was short-lived.

One of my professors loved to invite groups of students to dine at his residence, leading to one of my most hilarious memories. The professor himself was an introvert, coming across as near stoic. His lectures many times were, for me, exercises in semi-agony, as he dissected his subject matter in his extremely deliberate way. He was a gentle soul, always well prepared in the languages he taught. Many times, he seemed uncomfortable and overly accommodating in his interaction with students in class. I was surprised one day when I received an invitation to join several of my classmates in having dinner at his home. He was single, which probably contributed to his taking the largest room in his house and converting it to a library with rows of shelving for hundreds of books.

He had set a large dining room table and served a wonderful spaghetti dinner to something like seven or eight of us. It was what happened in the middle of the meal that I will never forget. As we were all enjoying chatting and laughing, I noticed the professor engaging in what I can only describe as a *"Pink Panther* move." In the movie *The Pink Panther*, bumbling detective Inspector Clouseau, played by Peter Sellers, has a hilarious way of sneaking around. His exaggerated movements act to call attention to his attempt to be subtle, bringing laughter by the audience.

We saw him get up from his chair and move with theatrical deliberateness towards a bathroom just off the dining room. He was seeking to be unnoticed, but, instead, he drew attention to himself. He disappeared, and the next thing we all heard were explosive sounds. Something epic was happening in that bathroom. We all tried to remain as collected as we could while dealing with the incongruity. Keeping up the banter and snickering while downing our spaghetti, the professor finally emerged. He then "Pink Panthered" his way back to his seat, unaware that a blowout for the ages had entertained us during dinner! None of us dared use that bathroom afterward!

During those days at Houghton, I formed a friendship with Roger Richardson. Roger was an art teacher at the college and was about my age. By then, I was in my mid-twenties. Roger was one of the youngest professors there. He was single, from Canada, and somehow, we connected. We spent many hours bouncing around important issues, like life on the island and dating.

I would say I dabbled in dating during the first two years. I met some attractive and sweet coeds, whom I occasionally would take to a campus event or to someplace off-island. At a 40th Reunion, a woman named Linda reminded me of going to a basketball game in Wellsville (the college men's team had to play games at the high school there because our little gym was too small). She had some tale about a "hairy" ride through a snowstorm as we drove the thirty miles back to campus.

As I have mentioned, there were many weekends when I drove home to visit mom and dad or Mom and Pop Harris. Mom Harris had become my confidant, as well as a spiritual mentor. I had many things, including my dating life (or lack thereof) I could discuss with her. I could always depend upon receiving helpful feedback from someone who seemed to understand the longings and confusion of a single guy traveling through his twenties seeking the right partner for life as a pastor.

Iron Sharpens Iron

As one person sharpens another. Proverbs 27:17

In spiritually coming Home, I was discovering an ever-expanding family. At Houghton, I took a big step in understanding that family members could be of one mind and the same Spirit without all thinking alike. I have previously mentioned two theological terms, "evangelical" and "Wesleyan." In my time at Houghton, these two dynamics more deeply shaped who I was becoming in God's family. They had begun to take root under the tutelage of Pop Harris. Pop's life, pastoral ministry, and preaching reflected a commitment to these themes and streams.

I found it interesting that the student body of Houghton College seemed to be made up of more Baptists than Wesleyans, even though it was affiliated with the Wesleyan Church. I discovered that Baptists thought differently than Wesleyans. This happened most intently during discussions with fellow students that sometimes became heated. We would go round-and-round about whether or not some people were pre-destined to go to hell or heaven. I became fairly proficient at marshaling Scripture that proved my point, that we have a choice. Connected with this question was whether or not salvation could be lost. Once we were saved were we always saved? Again, I found much Scriptural support for "backsliding" --falling away from faith.

My instruction and reading helped me to understand the larger theological differences. The acronym T.U.L.I.P. was used to describe what Baptists believed. Theologian, John Calvin, had developed this understanding of Scripture. Each of the letters in this acronym stood for these beliefs: Total depravity, Unconditional election, Limited atonement, Irresistible grace and Perseverance, or Preservation, of the Saints. Wesleyan Biblical interpretation, under the influence of John Wesley and Jacob Arminius before him, led to some major differences. Wesleyans took issue with everything but Total depravity. And even then, it was argued that Preventing, or Prevenient, grace kept humans from being as bad as they could be.

I would get into these prolonged discussions--or arguments-- with my Baptist brothers, emphasizing Scripture that supported conditional election, unlimited atonement, resistible grace and the possibility of being lost AFTER being saved. To my knowledge, I never won anyone over to my way of understanding, but I did sharpen my own theological thinking. And I came to realize that the love of the Spirit trumped any differences.

I mentioned elsewhere that I had the opportunity to explore diverse theologies during my Houghton days. I appreciated the fact that instead of straw men being set up in order to knock them down, students were encouraged to read theologies that were outside of the commitment of the college. However, the Evangelical stance of the college had played a part in my choosing to go there. Evangelical theology was fleshed out in that setting, and I came to understand that to mean an embracing of the Scriptures as Divine Revelation, inspired by the Spirit, and to be completely trusted for faith and practice.

Miracles found in both the Old and New Testaments were accepted as genuine supernatural occurrences, and not explained away. A personal commitment to Jesus Christ, which is what I had made at that altar rail on March 24, 1968 (and earlier in church in the Burg), was central to a personal faith.

I bounced my own commitment off what I was reading, and many times it appeared that these modern theologians had allowed their intellect to get in the way of a personal commitment and faith. Paul Tillich's philosophizing and using terms like, "God is the ground of our being" and "Stuck somewhere between the no more and the not yet," seemed a contrived way of legitimizing "antiquated" Biblical images, as well as a put-down of evangelical understanding. Explaining away miracles like the parting of the waters of the Red Sea, the feeding of thousands with a few loaves and fish, and the Resurrection, only confirmed to me that human intellectual arrogance had prevailed.

In stark contrast to this was the demonstration of warm evangelical faith on the part of my professors. I vividly remember my New Testament teacher, Professor Woolsey, standing humbly before faculty and students, comparing his life to the pillars in front of Wesley Chapel and confessing that his walk with Christ had become as dry as dust. He had been convicted by the preaching of one of our annual renewal leaders. On another occasion, Dr. Stephen Paine, the President of the college, and my Greek teacher, stood before our class and apologized to me personally for a harsh response to a question I had asked the day before. I was taken aback by this, and it affirmed the beauty of this special place into which the Lord had placed me for shaping.

Sartwell Creek

Sometime in the second semester of my junior year at Houghton I was asked by fellow student, Gary Greenwald, to consider serving as pastor of the Sartwell Creek United Methodist Church near Port Allegany, Pennsylvania. Gary, a senior, who had been serving the church for almost two years as a part-time pastor, knew me from Frewsburg. We both grew up there. He was several years younger but was a year ahead of me in college because of my delayed start. Gary described the congregation and setting to me. Knowing that I could use both the experience and compensation, I began the process of assuming responsibility for this little flock. I drove down and visited with the congregation. I also met with the District Superintendent of the Kane District. It took a while, but eventually I was issued a local preacher's license so that I could have some kind of official credentialing and preside at communion. I assumed the pastoral leadership of the congregation in June of 1971.

The one-room white clapboard church building was located about five miles south of Port Allegany. The drive from campus to the church involved 65 miles over mostly secondary roads. The setting was in an idyllic valley two miles up the Sartwell Creek Road off of Rt. 6, running between Port Allegany and Coudersport. Because of the distance from campus, I was invited to spend Saturday nights at the homes of members of the congregation, particularly when there was visitation needing to be done or meetings to be held.

The folks were immediately welcoming even with my inexperience. It didn't take long to feel at home with families by the name of Van Sickle, Jestes, Baker, Howard, Earnst, Lamphier, Tubbs, and others. Benny and Becky Van Sickle, a young couple, we're glad to have someone in "their age bracket." Boyd and Velma Jestes often had me join them and their boys for Sunday dinner in their home at the end of Card Creek. I loved Velma's homemade small curd cottage cheese. Their two sons helped make up our small youth group. The Bakers made sure I had a warm bed in which to sleep when I needed to spend the night. I can still hear Doris's voice as she asked me if I had everything that I needed to be comfortable. The second floor room I occupied had a small desk so that I could complete sermon preparation. It WAS cold in that room in the winter, and I picture myself near a frosted window under a pile of blankets, falling asleep going over the main points of the next day's message.

It was during this summer and final year at Houghton that I met a coed by the name of Shelley. She was a beautiful Christian woman, who was in her junior year. From a hamlet in Western Pennsylvania, she was a gifted musician, and was preparing for a career in teaching. We dated much of my senior year. She offered to sing and play the piano at the Sartwell Creek church on a number of occasions. Shelley, along with the congregation of country folk, received with grace, my unpolished praying and preaching. I still laugh about an occasion when I was praying and blurted out something about so and so, who had oral surgery, being able to "sink his choppers into some tough stuff." I think I heard a few snickers, and if I wouldn't have kept my eyes tightly closed, probably would have seen some eyes rolling. I know

Shelley was a huge blessing to those folks. I have never forgotten the warmth of her love and laughter during those days of taking that second plunge into the waters of ministry as a greenhorn pastor.

Local Preachers License

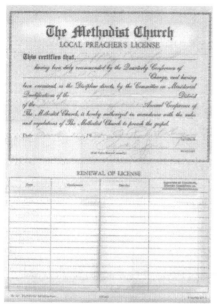

A source of great wisdom and encouragement during those days of serving the folks in Sartwell Creek were Rev. Jerry Lundeen and his wife, Ruth. Jerry was the pastor of the Port Allegany United Methodist Church. We shared the background of belonging to the Erie Conference of the Evangelical United Brethren Church prior to the merger with the Methodist Church in 1968. The Lundeens were friends of the Harrises, and Jerry became a mentor. I could go to him with any question I had regarding pastoral ministry. And I trusted Ruth with sharing with me spiritual insight regarding my personal journey. My wife, Bev, and I still see Ruth at the Bible Camp we have attended for many years and at Old Erie Conference Reunions.

Thankfully, there have been times when we have kept in touch with the folks in that congregation, even attending a reunion or two.

The bucolic scenes, created on early Sunday morning drives up the Sartwell Creek Road in the summer, when the

sun was burning through the mist that had settled in the valley, backlighting farm equipment left in the fields, remain etched in my mind.

A Decision

As my senior year progressed into the second semester, I began to feel some pressure as to where I would attend seminary. After all, graduation was coming in May! I was somewhat familiar with Asbury Theological Seminary from getting to know John Cooke, the pastor who had helped me with communion when I served the Pleasant Valley church. John and I had developed a friendship, and he encouraged me to "think Asbury." The Wesleyan theology taught there resonated with my evangelical shaping through my home church and Houghton.

But I was attracted to Perkins School of Theology at Southern Methodist University in Dallas, because of what I perceived to be "cutting edge" theological exploration. There were a number of noted Methodist scholars who taught there. Perhaps the foremost expert on John Wesley, Albert Outler, served as one of its professors. I considered myself a budding theologian.

In the spring of 1972, I packed my mustang* and headed for Dallas, Texas, where I had set up a meeting with the admissions office, as well as a tour of the campus. It was a long drive but worth every mile. On the way, I stopped in Tyler, Texas, to visit a friend from my years in Kansas. Texas was beautiful in the spring, and I enjoyed seeing the longhorn cattle in fields sprinkled with dogwood trees. When I arrived at the campus, it had been arranged for me to stay with a seminary student. The seminary proved to be everything I expected, and I was offered a full scholarship because of the quality of my work at Houghton, and because I would be an easterner among a student body made up of mostly westerners. On my drive home, the thrill of a venture like this filled my head and heart, interrupted only by a little detour I had arranged.

I hadn't been to the Crawford farm since I was nine years old, and since I was heading east, I wanted to stop and see what the old place looked like, as well as visit my grandmother, Vera. Things began to look familiar when I reached the road to the farm in Millard, just a few miles south of Kirksville, Missouri. Pulling into the driveway, which ran between the house and the main barn, I was taken aback by how much smaller everything looked. My boyish perspective had been replaced by that of a young man. I enjoyed my reunion with

Grandma Vera, who made sure I was fed as well as the barn cats. I got quite a laugh out of seeing her give them their daily helping of milk and hearing her say as they crowded the dish, "Durn cats!" I took a walk out into a large pasture amongst a small heard of heifers and reminisced about those days when I spent two weeks on the farm helping Grandpa Crawford with various chores, including slopping the hogs. I slept upstairs in the old brass spindle bed I had used as a boy. The night I spent there I experienced a strange, dragging sound above me. When I told Grandma about it the next morning, she took offense and was dismissive. A few weeks later she wrote to me, telling me that a family of raccoons had been discovered in the attic. A local farmer had to come and remove them. Apparently, a tree next to the house had served as a "ladder" to a hole just above a window.

I returned to the Houghton campus determined to complete the admission process to become a student at the Perkins School of Theology in Dallas, but something made me hesitate. I could not dismiss the question that had become embedded in my soul, "What about Asbury?" After all, it was a thriving place, known for preparing pastors like John Cooke, who were well-equipped both theologically and practically. And its ethos centered on a vital evangelical faith, rather than a theological smorgasbord, vaguely based on the Wesleyan approach. And so, I wrestled... hearing a still small voice that I had encountered the summer before, when I had attended the Bible Conference at Findley Lake in Western New York.

The conference was held at a camp that had been a long time sponsor of summer camping, first for the Evangelical United Brethren Church, and now for the United Methodist Church. The Bible Conference was thirty-five years old that summer (1971). Pop Harris had served for years as the Dean of this week-long camp held in July but had recently turned the leadership over to pastor Spurgeon Witherow, who liked to call me "Skirt Chaser." I guess he had taken notice of my obvious wife-hunting.

Reverend Witherow had scheduled for the evening preacher Dr. Dennis Kinlaw, long time Old Testament Professor at Asbury Seminary, but more recently, the President of Asbury College, located across the street from the seminary, in Wilmore, Kentucky. In a conversation I had with Dr. Kinlaw, I told him about my mulling over where to go for my seminary education. Listening intently, he broke into a smile, for which he was noted, as a way of expressing understanding. After hearing me out, he said to me, "Jeff, you need to be at Asbury." It was THAT voice, the voice of Dr. Kinlaw, I could not dismiss.

That voice became God's voice, enabling me to surrender my "plans" and submit myself to God's better judgment and providential leading. Peace came over the troubled waters of decision-making, the wrestling stopped, and I focused on completing the process towards acceptance at Asbury Seminary so that I could begin in September.

The Mustang and I in front of the barn.

*This Mustang had replaced my Buick Electra prior to my second year at Houghton. See the "Bookman" reflection.

KIP

Prior to my senior year, I took my meals in the dining room of East Hall on the campus--I bought the full board package. For a variety of reasons, I decided to buy only some of my meals on campus for my senior year. One of those reasons was that I had sampled the fare at the Houghton Inn, almost directly across from the Keith House, where I lived, and I had gotten to know the owner, whose nickname was "Kip."

James "Kip" Randall and his wife, Betty, had purchased the Inn in 1970. They lived in Castile, a small village north of Houghton, just off Rt. 19, near Letchworth State Park. The Inn had a restaurant downstairs and several rooms upstairs, where people could find a comfortable place to stay. Since there were motels in the area, occupants of the rooms typically were those who needed a place for a more extended period of time.

Like most small business owners, Kip, who ran the restaurant, was there most of the time and gave it personality. I remember him as a smallish man, who almost always wore a white shirt and spoke with a gravelly voice. He had a great sense of humor as he worked tirelessly at preparing and serving meals. Since the Inn provided the only restaurant along that part of the corridor that winds its way from the Pennsylvania line to Lake Ontario near Rochester, NY, it was a crossroads of sorts. In my taking lunch and dinner meals there, I met many interesting people, including an F.B.I.

agent, who compared the Inn's fare with his wife's cooking. Let's just say he preferred what he ate at the Inn.

Kip needed someone to help him with cleaning the restaurant after hours, so I assumed that role sometime during my senior year. I exchanged working those hours for meals. As my senior year came to an end and I was finishing my pastoral role at Sartwell Creek, I needed a place to stay. I had to vacate my room at the Keith House after graduation, and I didn't really want to move back to Jamestown for three months before beginning seminary at Asbury. So, I rented a room at the Inn. Kip saw an opportunity to get some relief from the evening hours that were part of a long day, and he employed me to run the place a couple of nights during the week. With a quick orientation, I became a short order cook and waiter, in addition to closing up and cleaning. Again, I was able to barter with Kip and trade running the restaurant for my room cost. A few memorable things happened during that experience.

One night, a couple stopped in and ordered jumbo shrimp. Not realizing that I needed to cook the shrimp, I served them right out of the refrigerator. I thought they looked funny, and after being embarrassed, I prepared them appropriately. On another occasion three ladies, whose meals I had prepared and served, left me a "tip." I found some change and a business card on the table after they left. The card said something like, "Here's a tip: Jesus saves." I was NOT pleased. Finally, an Ethiopian who had been a student at a nearby college but who needed a room for a couple of weeks during the transition, made it clear that he would NOT eat a hotdog, because "dogs had been used to provide the meat!" No amount of reasoning could change his mind. It probably didn't help that I kept breaking into laughter during my attempt to convince him otherwise.

One other thing happened that I will never forget. I noticed one night that there appeared to be gnaw marks on a pie that Betty had made. Sensing that this could be the sign of a rat's presence, I put out poison. A couple of nights later, I was in the kitchen preparing food when the woozy rodent appeared. It kept flopping over in trying to climb onto a lower shelf. I clubbed it with a broom handle and threw it out the back door of the restaurant. After that I saw no evidence of the varmints. Kip appreciated my work as an exterminator, asking me if I wanted a medal for my efforts.

Almost two weeks after I moved over to the Inn, the flood of 1972 occurred. Hurricane Agnes caused torrential downpours and overflowing rivers in the Southern Tier of New York State and northern Pennsylvania, flooding places like Corning and Elmira. The Genesee River, which snakes its way near Rt. 19 in that area, began to overflow its banks. The river was within easy walking distance from Houghton. I got so concerned that it could end up flooding the area where the Inn was located, that I threw all my books and belongings into my car and prepared to vamoose. Thankfully, it never happened. Homes like the Keith House across the road were spared damage, and business went on as usual at the Inn.

Kip, in his unique way, was a part of the fabric of life on the "island," a nearly seamless Christian academic community in a sea of Americana. Kip didn't fit the "Houghton mold," but he was an authentic, colorful, and precious person, who made a significant contribution to the larger community. I honor him and his wife who owned and ran the Houghton Inn for twelve years, 1970-1982. And I am grateful for the friendship we shared, particularly in that last year, prior to transitioning to Asbury Seminary, where the Lord would continue His work of preparing me for pastoral ministry.

ATS

I arrived at Asbury Theological Seminary (ATS) in late August, 1972, after a summer split between working for Kip at the Houghton Inn, and spending time at home. I had been assigned a room in the single men's Dorm, named Larabee Morris. Wilmore, Kentucky was... HOT. Our air conditioning was a fan in the window. My roommate was a student named Steve, who was an upperclassman. I don't remember much about him, other than that he was an easy-going guy, who loved to sit in our room strumming a guitar. Living with someone else hadn't happened since I was in the army, so it took an adjustment.

I immediately met and started to get to know other first year students with names like Tom Thomas, who also went by H.O.T., an acronym for Howe Octavius Thomas, and Charlie Spears. Tom was from Arizona and had graduated from the State University there. He had the look of Wild Bill Hickok and drove a Plymouth Valiant. He had grown up a Methodist and had a wacky sense of humor. Charlie was an Oklahoma boy, who had been saved out of the drug culture. He wore his hair long, and had a thick, shovel-blade-like beard. He had tales to tell about his former life and carried a gallon jug of drinking water around the dorm. His quick wit was punctuated by effusive praise that his drug use as a hippy hadn't "fried his brain." Both of these brothers-in-Christ's-arms were extremely serious about what we were there to do... and become. Kidding around was appreciated, but then it was time to get serious about class work and prayer.

The fact that Asbury College was across the street became important for most of the guys. We became aware that many a fine coed and well-formed Southern belles were housed there. I had no interest in that stuff because I was already focused on a fine woman, Shelley, whom I had begun dating during my senior year at Houghton. In fact, we became engaged during my first semester at Asbury. The twelve hour drive to see her made our being together difficult, but we managed a few times, and her parents were wonderful hosts during long weekends. A combination of factors resulted in the engagement being broken. It was one of the most difficult decisions I have ever made and extremely hurtful for both of us. However, I had come under an undeniable conviction that we were not making the right choice for a life's partner. I remember feeling like one of the world's biggest losers, who needed some major healing from dynamics that haunted me from the past. When I discussed this with my mom, she became exasperated, and exclaimed, "You're NEVER going to get married!" I have to admit that I wondered about this myself.

As time rolled on, I became immersed in my class work. This was a culture with one primary goal: preparing men and women to be pastors. Courses like Church History, Christian Ethics, Theology, New Testament Greek, Introduction to the New Testament, and Old Testament Biblical Studies demanded intense focus. This meant studying either in my room or in the campus library for hours every day. I had brought an old Smith-Corona typewriter with me from college and found myself pulling some all-nighters banging out required papers.

As always, I found it fascinating and sometimes amusing getting to know my professors. Most of them during this first year were cut from a similar mold. They were no-nonsense men, who could get fired up in class and sometimes "went to preaching." I gave one of them the nickname, "Wild" Bill Arnett. He taught theology and was always dressed in a suit. A reserved man, he claimed Christian perfection in a humble sort of way. It was entertaining for me when he went up on the balls of his feet, his voice rising to a crescendo, when making a point.

One could not escape from experiencing Dr. WANG! I write his last name in capitals, reflecting his habitual intensity. He was a Greek and New Testament teacher. His Introduction to the New Testament course was required of everyone. He was from Taiwan and had recovered from a near-death experience as a boy. Dr. Wang (pronounced "Wong" in English), expected words to be parsed correctly and exegesis to line up with his interpretation. Because of his Chinese background, he had trouble with saying "S" and "L." So, he would talk about "virgins" (versions) of the Bible and at least once he emphasized that Biblically speaking, when it came to women, men should "rook not rust" (look not lust). At one point, a fellow student, sitting in the front row, burst out laughing when Wong let loose with one of these. His brilliance was duly appreciated by most of us, and we felt like we had been profoundly baptized in an apologetic defense of the Gospel experienced under his tutelage.

There were other notable teachers during those first semesters at ATS. Dr. Kenneth Kinghorn fascinated students with his interpretations of the lives of formative figures in Church History like Martin Luther and John Wesley. Dr. Don

Joy taught Christian Education using a moral development perspective and believed that "all truth was God's truth, and we, as Christians, have the right to claim it." Dr. John Oswalt provided awe-inspiring insights into the Old Testament.

Of course, within the fabric of academia, there are inevitably less scintillating, but still memorable, dispensers of critical knowledge. One professor was so agonizingly deliberate in delivering his words during lectures that some of us thought he might fall asleep during his own lecture, as he clutched the lectern. Another made us soldier through Biblical studies, fending off boredom every step of the way. He recommended that students read a book titled *How to Read a Book*. This was intended to help us observe more carefully and deepen our study of Biblical texts. Another student, who, believe it or not, was from the Burg and also had attended Houghton College, read this book. Afterward, he said the following about the author: "He should have read a book about how to write a book, before he wrote a book about how to read a book!"

And so, my seminary phase was launched, and I became a part of a community of similarly focused brothers and sisters, who loved and supported one another as we journeyed together towards fulfilling our calling to be pastors.

Bookman

Part of my preparation for pastoral ministry involved being a book salesman. For two summers I sold books door-to-door for the Southwestern Company. I did this between my sophomore and junior year in college and

between my freshman and second year in seminary. I had at least two reasons for doing this. One reason was so that I could earn some badly needed money. The other reason was so that I could gain confidence in dealing with the variety of people I would encounter in congregations as a pastor. Also, I was comfortable with trying to get into people's hands the Bible-related books I would be selling: a Children's Bible Story Set, a Bible Dictionary, and the Nave's Topical Bible.

Attending sales school prior to being sent to the field was required. My first school included a hundred or so college students from all over the East who learned memorable sales mantras. For instance, we should roll out of the door in the morning, and even get into our car (if we had one), shouting, "I feel happy, healthy and terrific!" We were told that pounding on the car roof while shouting this could be REALLY inspiring! Preparing for the day, it was "helpful" to look at one's self in a mirror, and say, "You cute little booger you, don't you ever die!" These, of course, were to help inflate our confidence for a day of knocking on doors. We also practiced helping people say "yes" to our sales pitches. This always involved positive words and nodding. We were taught to avoid giving a potential customer the option of saying, "No." Every negative inquiry was to be met with, "I know what you mean but let me ask you this question." The pitch concluded with, "So how would you like to pay for these?"

Following a week of this psyche-bending, I was off, singing a song that had been drilled into us. It went like this: "It's a great day, to be a bookman, it's a great thing, I know. It's a great day to be a bookman, everywhere I go...o... o....o. Goodbye 'no', 'never.' Goodbye doubts and fear. It's a great day to be a bookman, and to be of good cheer!"

The first summer I was assigned the Los Angeles area, first to Norwalk, and then Artesia, California. I left my Buick Electra behind and rode with Dave and Mary Wyrtzen, fellow students at Houghton. For the most part, our long trek was uneventful, except for finding a small critter inhabiting a candy bar that I bought at a desert convenient store, somewhere between Phoenix, Arizona, and Los Angeles. Fortunately, we hadn't driven off, when I removed the wrapper from the Pay Day. When I showed the cashier, he told me to "go get another one," adding, "He didn't eat much."

It didn't take long to find accommodations in those communities, both of which contained a mixture of housing developments and huge dairy operations, and so we began cold-selling, door-to-door. Since I didn't have a car, I bought a used bicycle and attached my sales box to the handlebars. Each morning began with eating cereal and brushing my teeth, all the while engaging in self-psyching using the lingo and ditties we had learned in sales school. At 8 am, out the door I went. I remember asking myself, "How crazy is this, knocking on doors during the summer at this hour of the morning?!"

Overall it went pretty well. I encountered the usual rejections, having doors slammed in my face. But I met some wonderful people, including the Vandenbosches, who not only bought a Bible Dictionary, but invited me to stop by anytime, and have a sit on their front porch. It was during this time that I became so persistent in pursuing potential sales opportunities, I went into a fancy cow barn/milking parlor in Norwalk to talk to a farmer, who was involved in milking his cows. My exit was hastened when, after approaching the man, I got splattered with dung.

My roommate in California was a fellow Houghton student, who had also ridden with the Wyrtzens, but whose personal habits I found irritating, because of their unrelentingly repetitive nature. He ate the same cereal every morning and returned at the same time for lunch, always devouring a peanut butter and jelly sandwich. He never left for a day of knocking on doors without a shirt pocket protector full of pens. I simply had to adjust to having a partner who was boringly intense in his determination to succeed. My experience in the second year was to be completely different.

I made more than $3,000 that summer and was able to buy a 1966 Mustang to replace my used-up Electra. It was a "California car" with no rust. After having some dings removed and having it painted a powder blue by the renowned Earl Scheib, I drove it cross-country to Jamestown. I have a picture, taken in front of Mom and Pop Harris's, of me standing beside it, wearing the Mickey Mouse Ears I had obtained during a visit to Disneyland. This was my car until Bev, and I got married, and we decided to drive her much more practical car, a four-door Rambler. I gave the Mustang to my sister, Paula.

The second summer (1973) my territory was Petersburg, and then, Richmond, Virginia. I remember staying in what turned out to be a cockroach-infested apartment in Petersburg. It was not uncommon to get up in the night and experience the crunching of one of these critters under my foot. I found better accommodation when we moved to the Richmond area.

My roommate in Petersburg and Richmond was Mark. I don't remember where he was from, but he made a perfect salesman. He had a carefree aspect to his personality that enabled him to have fun dealing with all sorts of people. He would come home at the end of the day and entertain me with stories of some of the goofballs he met along the way. One night he had me believing that he was frightened out of his wits by someone whom he heard calling his name from behind in an ally. It began as a whisper, becoming louder the closer it got. He began to walk faster. Then Mark delivered the punch line: "I turned around and it was a dog with a speech impediment!"

But the most unforgettable tale involved a man who answered the door at the end of a long driveway. We had been instructed to never skip a house so with stubborn determination Mark made his way to the front porch. As he launched into his sales pitch, this man, notably irritated, threatened to get his gun! Mark, being the jovial type who loved to kid around, laughed it off. After another threat, and Mark not taking him seriously, he left the door, presumably to fetch a firearm. That was when Mark left his porch!

 It was during this summer that I had my two most memorable sales experiences. Upon walking up to a house, I noticed a gaping hole in the wall beside the door. I knocked on the door but ended up walking through the hole when invited in. You can believe that I didn't try to hard sell this struggling family. I had a wonderful conversation with them, sharing my personal faith journey and offering encouragement.

The other experience happened when, after waiting for a response to my knock one afternoon, I was abruptly greeted through a screen door by a frizzy-haired, barefoot man, wearing a ripped T shirt and shorts. He listened as I stumbled through my usual introduction: "Hi, I'm Jeff Crawford, just another one of those ole salesmen. You don't shoot em, hang em, or cut their tongues out around here do ya?" Immediately he got this deranged look on his face, bringing his hands together in a choking manner, and with what I hoped was feigned anger, he said, "NO! But I strangle them!!" Well, I burst into laughter but didn't spend much time in further dialogue, thankful that there was that screen door between him and me!

The folks I encountered during those experiences had a real part in helping shape my spiritual life and confidence. I knew that the variety of people I met selling door-to-door might mirror the fabric of a congregation. I rarely had fun doing this but made the most of it, because I knew it was good for me, and hopefully, my customers.

I never completely bought into the "rah, rah" sales pitch ditties, but they sure have entertained me over the years since I completed my Bookman days!

Some Anomalies

It wasn't long before I experienced some anomalies around the campus of Asbury Seminary. There was a spotted dog named "Governor," probably a mixed breed, which ran the grounds. He would suddenly trot through the area behind the Administration Building, sniffing and lifting his leg at "approved" places. One time, I saw him with blood over much of his body. I wondered what kind of fight he had

been in. If Charlie Speers could, he would stick out his foot and say, "LOOOOOK." I have no idea why he did this, but it made me laugh and added to the mysterious presence of this dog. We never knew to whom he belonged or where he came from. We would see him, and taking Charlie's cue, we would say, "Governor, LOOOOK." I called him, "Governor, the Corny Dog."

In that same location, behind the Administration Building, steam rose out of the ground. There was really no vent there. It surfaced through a crack or some imperfection in the pavement. It was a wonder. We could never figure out where it came from other than surmising that there must be a leak in a pipe below, and somehow the steam found its way out. Our "theory" was that it was there to remind us, who lived in the "Holy City" Wilmore with its

Christian college and theological seminary, we were really not that far from hell after all.

Another anomaly involved the occasional "underpants raids." Even in the early to mid-seventies, panty raids were still happening on some college and university campuses.

These were events where a group of male students would gather outside of a women's dorm and chant, "give us your panties... give us your panties." Asbury Seminarians would have never thought of trying this on the campus of Asbury College across the street. The college ethos was marked by the Wesleyan holiness tradition, which meant there were strict rules regarding dating and what women could wear. But a strange twist occurred one night.

I was stunned when I heard women's voices calling for... our pants! A group of coeds from the college had crossed Main Street and stood below the second and third floor windows of our single men's dorm. I interpreted that as a desire for our skivvies. I had a pair of cherished boxer shorts decorated with hearts, and in a moment lacking in sanity, out they went. I only remember that happening once.

By the way, the college guys didn't cotton to us seminarians raiding "their" attractive coeds, and too often making them our wives. We came to refer to the campus on the west side of the street as "Canaan Land, the land of milk and honey(s)." It was the place where many of us thought we could find a fine date, if not a life's partner. More about that later...

There were three or four of us who loved to get into "costume" on Halloween. We were blessed to have a kind of "artist in residence." His name was Jeff, and he had been an art teacher prior to coming to the seminary. He helped us create some funny get-ups so that we could go to the college campus and "treat" the ladies. Now THAT we did do in front of dorms, no panty raids, though. One Halloween our artist brother crafted big stovepipe hats that three of us, John Wright, Mel Vostry and I, pulled over our faces and chests. He painted faces on our bellies, using our belly buttons as mouths. We then hooked shirts and ties to our waists, with only a small part of our legs, as well as our feet, being visible. So, we looked like very small "people," wearing massive hats. The only problem that occurred was trying to see clearly out of the small eye holes in the hats. An unforgettable mishap occurred when the three of us, plus Tom Thomas, who had pulled a carved out pumpkin over his head, were making our way across a dimly lit quad after visiting a couple of women's dorms. A park bench got in the way and two of us ended up on our actual faces.

While the seminary was more liberated than the college from rules that governed lifestyle, there were still vestiges of past rigidity. There was a sign which hung on the fence of our tennis courts that read, "No shorts, no Sunday sports!" So we took it upon ourselves to collect every piece of sports equipment we could find and had someone take our picture standing around the sign, each of us with an item for a respective sport and wearing shorts! We thought it was funny, but how would anyone know if it was Sunday or not? We posted it anyway!!

We could have been called "The Breakout Brothers," as we sought relief from the intensity of our studies. This involved a number of harmless dorm pranks, like short sheeting a bed or strategically placing water above a door to surprise someone with an instant "baptism." The bathroom between rooms shared by four of us had a poster above the toilet displaying a "recycler"–a toilet with pedals so that the toilet paper on the wall behind it could be... recycled?

Occasionally, we would head for Lexington, a fifteen-mile drive through Kentucky horse country, and enjoy eating at McDonald's or some other fast-food place. Once in a while we would splurge and have strawberry pie at Jerry's Restaurant. Tom Thomas often drove his Plymouth Valiant with its push-button transmission. He inevitably morphed into the "Valiant Bombardier," using whipping motions to make the car "go faster." Go figure!!

I included a photograph taken of me standing in the hallway of Larabee, wearing long johns, with heating lamp goggles covering my eyes and topped with a woman's sun hat. Creating humorous get-ups in addition to Halloween was not uncommon. The most hilarious was Tom's "half a pair of pants." It was a pair of chap-like pants that he put on over his underwear. He looked totally normal coming towards you, but then... It is little wonder that these were four of the most enjoyable years of our lives! And Charlie wasn't even trying to be funny when he wore the same predictable outfit every day in the dorm and elsewhere.

It was that less-than-white T shirt that was too small for his elongated torso, boot-cut jeans, and motorcycle boots, although I never knew of him to ride one. It was one of those booted feet that he stuck out, whenever he saw Governor, the Corny Dog, and said, "LOOOOOOK!"

Unfinished Business

During my second year in seminary, I decided to "cram three years into four." That is, I opted to make it a four year experience rather than the normal three. I began to sense that trying to complete an average of fifteen hours of course work a semester so that I could finish the required 90 hours in three years, was just not going to be enjoyable, nor was it going to equip me in the way I thought necessary. I needed to work and wanted to have time to relax and absorb what I was learning. A factor in this was the job I acquired at Rogers Restaurant in Lexington.

I also became aware that I needed to work on some damaged emotions from the abuse I had endured at the hands of my biological father. * The Lord's influence in my decision to attend Asbury became strikingly clear, as I realized that I had been placed in the middle of a healing community. The connections I formed with my fellow students and professors, and the preaching of Dr. David Seamands, pastor of the Wilmore United Methodist Church, helped expose destructive dynamics that were impeding my maturation as a Christian.

There was a point during this second year when I fell under a pall of guilt. There seemed little I could do about the constant condemnation that nagged my soul. In trying to assuage this, I became obsessive. I would play little games, setting up a series of actions I needed to take, in order to feel absolved. I prayed, and the heavens seemed as brass. I couldn't understand it, but it dogged my steps. It was during this time that a group of students I met with for prayer and fellowship, and with whom I could be completely honest, affirmed their love for me. They assured me that God was still there and loved me, even if I couldn't sense it.

God used the ministry of Dr. Seamands as well, during this time of upheaval in my spiritual life. The Wilmore church drew many students and faculty from both the college and seminary. Dr. Seamands had a gift of bringing psychological insights into his Biblical preaching. I remember one of my professors saying that he "puts people on the couch every Sunday." One of his areas of focus was on helping people with damaged emotions. In fact, he would later write a book by that title.

During a series of sermons focusing on the nature of God, Dr. Seamands emphasized God's fatherly nature. He declared that God was NOT a celestial perfectionist, looking over the banister of heaven to see who was not measuring up so that He could punish them. Rather, the Heavenly Father was full of grace and compassion, understanding the imperfections, frailty, and faults of His people, and desiring to enable healing. It began to dawn on me that I had been projecting the nature and actions of a broken human father upon God.

At about this same time I was learning in my reading for classes what John Wesley, the founder of Methodism, taught about conscience. In his observation there were four types of consciences. The first and second of these, the "good" and closely aligned "tender" conscience, lined up with Biblical truth and brought one to a healthy conviction when falling short of loving God and mankind. The third was a "hardened" or "seared" conscience. It was reflected in one who felt no condemnation when failing to love God and mankind. The fourth type was the "scrupulous" conscience, provoking unnecessary self-condemnation and guilt. In modern analysis this is sometimes connected with obsessive and compulsive behavior. This last one described me.

A profound healing revelation occurred, when the Lord brought all of this together, and I realized that the God who had summoned me to be His child and to serve as a pastor to His children was a loving parent who wanted wholeness for his people. It struck me that I had already experienced this in my stepdad and mom and in the Harrises, as well as in so many others within the family of God. It became obvious that I was in the Asbury community for more than just an academic preparation for pastoral ministry.

I began a journey towards forgiving my biological father when I stopped to visit him and his family in Mesa, Arizona, on the way back from selling books in California in 1970. Mom Harris had written to him, letting him know that I was preparing for pastoral ministry. We engaged in a few brief phone conversations during my college and seminary years. Visits to spend time with him occurred after Bev and I married and had begun our family. By then he had moved to Independence, Missouri. These visits were in conjunction with spending time with Uncle Jack and his family in Kirksville, Missouri. Although he never offered an apology for his abusive behavior, I could do no less than extend to him the same love and forgiveness that I had experienced from the Lord of Life. My uncle and I cleaned out his apartment when he had a stroke on Christmas Day, 2002, and needed extended care.

He died one year later in 2003. The best thing to come from my reconnecting with my biological father was getting to know my half-brother, Carl. Carl was the fruit of a second marriage and is a wonderful Christian and a delight to be around.

Rogers Restaurant

As I began my second year of seminary, it became clear that I needed a boost in my income to keep me from going too far into debt. I had already taken out some student loans for college, and I didn't want to add any more than absolutely needed. A student in our dorm had found a job as a busboy at the oldest restaurant in Lexington, and he recruited me to work there. Rogers Restaurant, a beloved eatery in town, known for its menu of southern favorites like lamb fries, country ham with redeye gravy, and stewed tomatoes, had employed a string of Asbury Seminarians. George Rogers, the founder and owner, liked this because he knew he could depend on men from the seminary being punctual, responsible and, well, nice guys. I drove the fifteen miles to the restaurant on Broadway two or three times a week, beginning work in the late afternoon, working until closing time at 9:30.

I can still picture eighty-year old Mr. Rogers, with a cigar stub in his mouth, slicing steaks on a free standing cutting board. There was a sweet, smallish black woman, who was responsible for the salads, and a couple of guys who did dishes, Bill and Jackson. Jackson was a jovial black man who permeated his dishwashing with comments about his love for fishing. I can hear him tell me that "Saturday, I'm goin feeshin!" Busboys pitched in wherever we were needed, but mostly we "bused tables," cleaned off dirty dishes, replaced the tablecloths if needed, and reset tables. We also helped waitresses deliver meals to customers when busy.

There were two waitresses who had worked for Mr. Rogers for several years. They could be salty, but they respected the seminarians who worked there. Caroline had the habit of pointing to her cheek and asking me for "a little sugar" when I arrived for work. She had fun waiting to see if I would give her a kiss. I usually obliged with a peck on the cheek. There was something about Louise, the other waitress, who reminded me of my aunt Alverta. She was sweet and lovable. They both referred to me, more often than not, as "Darlin" or "sugar."

Because of all the frying that was done in the kitchen, I arrived back at the seminary smelling like a French fry. At least that was the description I used. And my buddies in the dorm usually agreed. It was always a tedious drive back to campus after carrying tubs of dirty dishes to the kitchen for several hours. Route 68 was narrow and winding. Mailboxes always seemed too close, inspiring the poem I have included in this book. Snaking my way to Wilmore, the white fences of the horse farms gleamed on moonlit nights. About ten miles out there was the highly anticipated "dead man's curve," with its billboard that read, "PREPARE TO MEET THY GOD."

Prior to my last year of seminary, Mr. Rogers sold the restaurant to two couples. One of the couples, the Ellingers, was hands-on in the management of the restaurant. Charles Ellinger was on the dental faculty of the University of Kentucky. He was present as often as he could be. His wife took over staff scheduling and oversaw finances. They appreciated the seminary busboy pipeline, and at one point, all the busboys were from Asbury.

Because of Mr. Ellinger's connection to the University of Kentucky, my dream of attending a basketball game was realized. I attended the last home game that the Wildcats played in Memorial Coliseum on the campus. The next year they moved to Rupp Arena in Lexington.

My love of the Kentucky Wildcats was cemented when the team began coming into the restaurant once a week for their evening meal. It was always a thrill to see 6'10" guys bend over to fit through the entrance. There was a side room where tables were put together to accommodate the players. I normally helped serve this hungry crew and found that they were a gracious and jovial group. Usually, one of the assistant coaches accompanied them, but Coach Joe B. Hall joined them on occasion. In fact, the men who made up the team at that time formed the nucleus of the National Champions of 1978.

Being a busboy was somewhat humbling and taught me some important lessons in how to serve. It provided me with a great opportunity and challenge to share a distinct and loving witness to the Jesus who had welcomed me Home. I will never forget being invited by Louise to her family Thanksgiving dinner. And before he sold the restaurant, Mr. Rogers personally expressed his gratitude to me and the other seminary busboys by making us special guests at a Prime Rib Roast in his beautiful home on the edge of Lexington.

MAILBOX

Spindly

Legged

Metal Mouth,

Wagging

Its

Tin Tongue

At

All

Passersby.

Seems like

It would choke

On all that paper,

Or

On those

Anxious fists,

Thrust

Down its

Throat,

Seeking
Its
Content.

Oblivious,
Yet
Intimidating,

Daring proximity
With that...
Tireless Tongue!

Dating and Dorm life

I was moving into my late 20's, trying to remain calm regarding my lack of a serious relationship. After all, what single seminarian, twenty-seven or twenty-eight years old and anticipating a life as a pastor, liked the idea of being single? Not this man! It's not that I wasn't trying. As often as I could, I found my way over to the college campus and its snack bar. Remember, we single seminarians called the west side of the main street, "Canaan, a land flowing with milk and honey(s)?" My alleged reason for visiting the snack bar was to enjoy a cup of coffee in surroundings that included pretty coeds. But I was hunting for the One, whom I could "look at across the breakfast table for the next forty years." That memorable phrase came from one of David Seamand's sermons.

As I mentioned in another reflection, there were many fine looking southern belles on the campus of Asbury College. I connected with one whom I called the "Hotlanta Hot Cake." She was a vivacious blond from Atlanta, Georgia. I took her to an event or two and enjoyed her energy and sense of humor, but eight years age difference and a lack of personality-fit bothered me. She was barely out of her teens, and I was an "old" experienced veteran, in more ways than one.

I also dated a couple of attractive seminarians. One was studying for a Masters in Christian Education. She was also from Georgia, and I visited her home on one occasion, staying with friends of her family. The other was preparing to be a pastor. It didn't take long to know in both relationships that there was just not going to be that "breakfast table" attraction.

Meanwhile, I was engaged in prayer in the dorm. We had a group of guys who got together on occasion to pray for things, including a life's partner. I just could not understand the approach that some of them took. With much importunity, they would ask the Lord to provide them with the love of their lives. Since I saw little engagement with women on their part, it appeared that they expected Him to open a fissure in the ceiling and drop her into their arms! I rolled my shut eyes, but I knew that prayer WAS critical to discernment and... patience.

Patience was one of my issues. I wasn't at a point of panic, but I could sense it coming. Thankfully, the whole culture in which I was immersed, as well as my Spiritual parents in Jamestown, counseled patience. The Scriptures urged trust, which is certainly a component of patience. In every way possible, I opened my life to biding my time, trusting that the Lord knew what was best when it came to giving me the "desires of my heart." I can say that a kind of peace settled over the anxiousness of my soul.

My other issue was perfectionism. I didn't have a written list of what I looked for in a wife, but I had given this much thought. I knew that as I got older, certain expectations were calcifying. I also saw this as a residual dark dynamic from the fathering I had experienced as a child. I will never forget a conversation I had with mom Harris. We had enjoyed a fish fry on one of my extended stays at home on a break from seminary. A frequent topic of conversation with her was my dating life. She asked me what I expected in finding a marriage partner. I noted a laundry list of gifts and abilities, including playing the piano. She looked at me and exclaimed, completely out of character, "Who the hell do you think you are?!" We both burst out laughing, but a point had been made.

Finally, in our dorm, my good friend, and eventual roommate, Tom "HOT" Thomas, had created a list he called "HOT'S Sure Shots." This list contained the names of a number of us single

seminarians who lived in Larabee Morris. If you were on this list and nothing much was happening date-wise, your name was at the bottom. You moved up the list as you established a relationship, and things became more serious. Engagement meant ascending to the top and marriage bumped you off the list. Let's just say that I spent much time as a "Larabee Loser," a moniker we created for dateless dorm guys. That is until THAT day and beyond.

"Hot Tom" and I in 1999

The DW

I mentioned previously, that I had decided to "cram three into four." During my second year of seminary, also known as the Midler year, I concluded that I wanted to enjoy my journey more and absorb as much as I could in preparing for pastoral ministry. I also needed to work part time. So it made sense to extend this experience to four years, rather than the traditional three, and reduce my course workload.

It was while I was deeply engaged in the first semester of my third year, that the world seemed to stop for a few minutes. I was returning from the college snack bar, when I was thunderstruck by the beauty of a woman whom I saw standing across the street. Everything around us seemed to blur, except for a corridor of the most wondrous light between us. It was as though she had stepped out of some dream into reality. Then she was gone... from my sight, but not from my mind. I knew I had to gaze upon the wonder of this dream woman again, but how and where?

Asbury College had a fall renewal series similar to that of Houghton College. I enjoyed attending the services in the campus chapel. One night I was seated in the balcony, which was shaped like a horseshoe. As I scanned the congregation, looking for the presence of the stunning mystery woman I had seen, I spotted her! She was sitting across the chasm from me, on the other side of the balcony. From that point on, I began referring to her as the DW - "Dream Woman." I HAD to find out who she was. But how?

I don't remember how I discovered the dorm where she lived, but once that happened, I described her to a Dorm Mother (they had those for the women's dorms at the college). She told me that she thought I was talking about a woman by the last name of Davis, which was also this woman's name by marriage. So, I had that bit of information, but that was it-- until an encounter that turned my world upside down.

My seminary dorm-mates had probably gotten tired of me detailing the little bit of information I had about this woman. They knew I referred to her as the "DW." I had managed to describe her to them enough so that they were able to identify her one night while we were studying in the library. I was trying to concentrate on something else for a change, when John Wright and HOT Thomas came to me, and asked me if I had seen who just came into the library. I said "no." They responded, "The DW, we think!" I then engaged in a feverish search of the library, all three floors, when I saw her exit from a first floor restroom. This was really the first time I laid eyes on her close-up, and everything that I had observed from a distance was confirmed. I was overwhelmed by her indescribable loveliness. In a euphoric state, I followed her to the third floor, where I observed the study carrel she occupied. Now what was I supposed to do?

Sitting at a round table, just west of where the DW was perched, John, HOT, and I entered into deep scheming regarding how I could introduce myself to her. We thought of ridiculous ploys like accidentally—on purpose—creating a "moment," by pulling books off the shelf near where she sat or "tripping" over the desk leg. Nothing made sense until I said I would just have to "suck it up," and walk over and introduce myself. I was never so nervous in my life.

In a swirl of emotions that made me light-headed, my heart audibly pounding, I took the few steps needed to reach her. Leaning over the back of the carrel, beholding for the first time those green eyes as she looked up at me, I spoke words to this effect: "Excuse me, but is your last name Davis?" When she said, "yes," I asked her for her first name. She told me, "Beverly." I then told her my name, sharing with her that I had seen her on the college campus and wanted to meet her.

My nerves began to calm as we chatted briefly, telling each

other a bit about ourselves. I discovered that she was an older student who had come to Asbury from Ohio in order to complete work for a bachelor's degree in Social Work. She had been working for Marathon Oil Company in Findlay, Ohio, and was previously married to her high school sweetheart. The six-year marriage hadn't worked, and its dissolution had led her back to the church of her youth and into a vital relationship with Jesus Christ. I mentioned to her that I had served in the army for three years and was preparing to be a pastor, after spending four and a half years completing college.

Our first conversation ended with me inviting her to attend an evening church service at the Wilmore United Methodist Church. I knew if I didn't ask her for a date, this could be the last time we connected. She accepted, and the woman of my dreams became a reality. I was twenty-nine years old and she was twenty-seven.

Ecstasy

I t felt like I had fallen in love with Beverly Poe Davis from the day I laid eyes on her walking on the campus of Asbury College. I couldn't believe I had this beauty riding beside me in my Mustang as we drove the quarter of a mile to church on that first date. The Wilmore United Methodist Church had evening services, and I always found something to write about during one of Dr. Seamand's sermons. In fact, I kept a notebook full of his Biblical insights. However, that night, I could have cared less about taking notes. My mind was on less spiritual things, like wondering what she thought of me, and was I going to say and do the right things.

After the church service we drove into Lexington for a piece of strawberry pie at Jerry's restaurant. Bev said that she had come over to the seminary library the night we met because it provided a less distracting place to study for an exam. THAT made me burst out laughing. That night began a journey of getting to know each other. This journey got interrupted by Christmas break. I would not see her for a month or so, but thoughts of her occupied a major part of my waking hours. I finished ringing bells for the Salvation Army in Auburn, New York, spent a couple of weeks at home with my family and Mom and Pop Harris, and I was back in Wilmore, anticipating deepening my relationship with Bev.

A humorous thing happened in January 1975. She had come to the seminary campus center so that we could play racquetball. We had new facilities and multiple courts. While we were playing, and I was trying to impress her with my athletic prowess, I hit myself in the forehead with the racket. I had taken a roundhouse swing at the ball and opened up quite a gash across my left eyebrow. While I was bleeding like the proverbial stuck pig, Bev drove me to an emergency room in Lexington, where I had to try to explain how this happened. This incident provided us with many laughs as our love for one another took root.

A dynamic we had to deal with was the Asbury College code of ethics regarding appropriate dress and acceptable behavior involving men and women. At that time coeds were prohibited from wearing pants to class and during normal campus activities. When I took Bev on an off-campus date, she would have to change into pants. I remember Dr. Don Joy, Christian Education and Moral Development professor at the seminary, questioning this approach. He asked why college officials thought it more appropriate for women, sitting in a mixed class, to wear more revealing skirts and dresses rather than pants.

We had to deal with that, but even more frustrating was what happened one evening as Bev and I sat in the admittedly dimly lit balcony of the chapel, praying, and reading Scripture. A college student, identified as a "Chapel Checker," told us that couples were not allowed in the balcony. We knew that the college was trying to guard against something unseemly occurring, but we were older than the typical student and felt it humiliating, as well as insulting.

The impending arrival of Valentine's Day provided me with a creative way to express my love for Beverly. I used red construction paper for Valentine's card base. I then glued blue velveteen cloth onto the paper, cut out four small hearts in a flower petal configuration. I also etched a flower stem. A red Valentine flower then showed through, gracing the front of this card. I then used the four hearts cut out from the velveteen to create flower petals for the envelope. I filled the inside of the card with a romantic verse, which flowed from the passion I could not contain. If she did not know it by then, this confirmed my love for her.

An interesting way that I found to release the passion I felt for her occurred through a class I was taking. One of my favorite teachers was Dr. John Oswalt, a professor of Old Testament Studies and Semitic Languages. In fact, I took something like seventeen hours of Hebrew and Old Testament Biblical courses from him. It so happened that during this semester we were studying Song of Solomon in a Hebrew class. Since this book involves an intimate look at the love between King Solomon and his beloved, I became creative for a project I was expected to complete. Bev and I audio-taped our speaking the Biblical dialogue between these lovers, and I played it in class as a part of the assignment. I don't remember my grade, but Dr. Oswalt and the class got quite a lot of enjoyment out of it.

Speaking of my expression of passion, this was an area where I needed some help. Prior to meeting Bev, I had traversed a period of time which I believed was intended to enable me to get my priorities straight. I had sought to discipline my thoughts and become more single-eyed in my passion for Christ, understanding that I must be patient with regard to finding a life's companion. Wild horses were raring to be released when I fell in love with Bev. She was the one who set boundaries and kept them with an iron-clad determination. I marveled at how a previously married woman could be so disciplined. This part of our relationship served to show me the purity of her heart. Biblical parameters for intimacy were not to be compromised. There was ONE who held first place in her life. There were many times during that year of dating when my hand was grasped and moved to a safe place, as we physically expressed our love for one another.

As that second semester of my third year moved along, we began having serious thoughts of marriage. My perfectionism reared its ugly head more than once, causing me to question things like whether or not I would be satisfied with Bev's cooking, her fit as a pastor's wife, and even if our sex life would be fulfilling. Fortunately, Dr. Don Joy, from whom I took several courses in moral development, became my sounding board. I spilled my uncertainties in his office, the campus dining room over a cup of coffee, and even in his home. I had divulged to him my background, including my home life as a child, and he was in tune with my nervousness in giving up my freedom. One time he said to me, "Look, if you really love Beverly, you need to commit to her no matter what, and trust that the Lord is in this."

As that year of seminary came to a close, I knew I could not imagine my future without my Dream Woman, Beverly. But there was one issue I had to confront, and it led to two months of pure agony.

Agony... But God

In that very first conversation with Beverly, with me leaning over the back of the study carrel in the seminary library, she had made me aware that there was a previous marriage, ending in a divorce. At that point, her being a divorcee was a minor blip on the screen. I had never been so swept off my heels like this by a woman. But after six months of getting to know each other and serious thoughts of marriage, this became an issue of struggle.

I began to wonder if a pastor should marry someone who had been divorced. Would the Lord bless such a relationship? Bev and I had had some conversation around this, but I didn't want to dwell on it with her and turn her off. I counseled with Mom and Pop Harris. Pop encouraged me to take a healthy approach to seeking and finding God's direction using Scripture, the wisdom of other Christians, reason, and sanctified intuition. He taught that these were like lights which guided a ship into the safe harbor. Mom reminded me that Bev was a "new creation in Christ." Dr. Joy offered support, while at the same time questioning the depth of my struggle, knowing how much I loved her. My seminary brothers empathized with what was becoming a point of agony. My Bishop, in a visit to the seminary, encouraged me to really think about this and resolve it in my own mind.

As the end of that third year was looming, I had a decision to make. I knew I could not consider marriage until I resolved this issue. To this day, the most difficult thing I have ever had to do was to tell Bev that I was going to have to have some time to wrestle with whether or not I could marry her. She was returning to Findlay, Ohio, for the summer, and I was going to remain in Wilmore, finding work with the owners of Rogers Restaurant. Fortunately, she was understanding, and had the confidence that this would all work out in the Lord's time.

Looking back, I agonized my way through two months of what felt like the hottest summer on record, renting a small apartment with no air conditioning at the top of a three-story building, doing odd jobs for the Ellingers, in addition to my busboy responsibilities. I spent many restless nights wondering why the Lord would bring such a beautiful woman into my life, only to deprive me of a life with her. But I was willing to do what I had to do in order to be in harmony with His will for my life. There were a few phone conversations between us, and we exchanged some letters, but communication was kept at a minimum, as excruciating as this was. I was never so miserable in my life.

The Wilmore United Methodist Church was a place of refuge during this time. Sometime in July, Dr. Victor Hamilton, Old Testament Professor at Asbury College, filled the pulpit for Dr. Seamands while he vacationed. One Sunday, Dr. Hamilton used for his Biblical focus the 10th chapter of the book of Acts. He unpacked a vision the Apostle Peter had while praying on his rooftop. As he prayed, Peter became hungry and fell into a trance. In a vision, Peter sees a sheet let down from heaven full of unclean animals. He then hears a voice saying, "Rise, Peter, kill and eat." Peter resists, saying, "I have never eaten anything impure or unclean." The voice then speaks to him and says, "Do not call anything impure that God has made clean." This happened three times. God was preparing Peter to receive emissaries from the Roman centurion, Cornelius, with an invitation to visit his home.

As I sat in the pew that Sunday, the Lord spoke to me. His word to me that day was unmistakable and overwhelming. Beverly was a new person. He had cleansed her from the brokenness of that previous relationship. I was never to view her as anything less than a pure and whole person in Him. He was setting me free to take her as my wife and life's partner. Tears of joy replaced those of my agony. I could not wait to get to a phone so that I could share with her the relief, and release, that I felt.

Looking back, I have thought many times about how the idea of an unappeasable, killjoy God, like my biological father, looking over the banister of heaven for anyone who looked like they were enjoying life, so that He could find fault and yell, "Cut it out!" played a part in my hesitation. I still had much to learn about a compassionate Father who only wants the best for His children, and who heals from brokenness.

Camp Prayer Unlimited

In my conversation with Bev after that life-altering Sunday, she invited me to meet her at a Christian camp in the heart of Ohio. It was called "Camp Prayer Unlimited" and was created as a way for people to draw closer to God by gaining a greater understanding of the power of prayer. I remember pulling into the campgrounds, set amidst an ancient grove of oak trees, containing a number of white cabin-type buildings that surrounded a larger assembly building. The starkness of the area around this stand of trees made this seem like an oasis in the desert.

Beverly was there to meet me, and we fell into each other's arms. I intended to never again relinquish that embrace, signaling my arrival at my true home in this world. I was overwhelmed with the reality of my dream coming true, the desire of my heart being granted. The gracious presence of the Lord was near palpable as we held each other for a time. When later that day, sitting under one of those massive oaks, I proposed, I could hardly believe my own voice. "Beverly, would you be my wife?" was met with, "Yes!" It was a warm August Saturday, and the thought reverberated through my being that I had just made the second most important decision I would ever make.

My wife-to-be had been a rock through my agonizing ordeal. I discovered more about her character during this wrestling. The combination of her strength of personality and the depth of her faith kept her steady as she bided her time. She had little doubt that the Lord would lead me out of my uncertainty and into a life-long intimate partnership with her. We both realized that ours was a "match made in heaven." The Lord's timing and plan made us laugh. Bev hadn't been looking for someone with whom to share a life that night in the library when I abruptly entered her world. And the idea of being a pastor's wife was about as far-out as any thought.

As I said, the camp was focused on prayer. The leadership and campers came from a particular theological perspective. Charismatic theology had swept into the mainstream church and brought new life. It was centered on the ministry of the Holy Spirit and emphasized that the same demonstration of power present in the first century church was available, and intended, for the 20th century, almost two thousand years later. Bev had been helped with healing from the brokenness of her divorce through the ministry of charismatic Christians, and I found my own faith refreshed through this emphasis on the present power of the Holy Spirit.

There were some extremes that I witnessed during the time we spent at this week-long camp. There was teaching on expelling demons that involved people coughing them out. While I took issue with that, the overall emphasis on being filled with love for the Lord and others, and taking authority over personal destructive dynamics, resonated with my understanding of Scriptural teaching. I will always be grateful for our engagement at Camp Prayer Unlimited, nestled in that grove of oaks in the middle of Ohio in August of 1975.

We also set the date for our wedding. We would be married on December 27, during our Christmas breaks from college and seminary.

This old bachelor had waited long enough, and we both wanted to spend our last few months in Wilmore enjoying marriage, before my graduation and the big move to our first appointment in western New York.

The Wedding

The months following our engagement at Camp Prayer Unlimited were focused on wedding preparations. Yes, college and seminary classes began in early September, but our lives were overflowing with anticipation for December 27. Bev and I worked on a budget, fully aware that our income as students meant that austerity was crucial. Thankfully, I had my part-time job at Rogers Restaurant busing tables and was going to earn a few hundred dollars ringing bells for the Salvation Army in December. Bev had some savings from her work at Marathon Oil Company prior to coming to Asbury College, and she was a seamstress of note. She began work on what would be her beautiful wedding gown.

As the fall progressed, a wonderful wedding shower was held in Findlay. We received many practical gifts with which to begin our life together. We secured Bev's home church for our venue. I bought a suit for $100 and wedding rings for $140. We created cards that had the invitation overlaying a photograph of us. All of the other details fell into place, and we were within our $2,700 in resources.

Money seemed sufficient, but manpower remained as a concern. My best friend and roommate, Tom Thomas, was unable to serve as my best man. He needed to return to his home in Arizona for the Christmas holidays. Fortunately, another good friend, Wayne Hepler, was more than willing. He was a seminary classmate whom I had gotten to know, and he and his wife, Patty, had opened their home to Bev and me on several occasions. Barry "Praise God" Bennett and Dale Winslow, seminary friends, agreed to serve as groomsmen/ushers. Bev had no such issue, because the wedding was occurring in her hometown of Findlay, Ohio, and she had many friends who lived and worked there.

Those were exciting days as we put our plans in place. I took Bev home so that I could introduce her to my family and Mom and Pop Harris. Pop agreed to share the responsibility of marrying us with Bev's pastor, Rev. J. Paul Jones. He worked with us around putting the service together, including writing our vows. We were surrounded by the love of so many friends and family members. I had already become acquainted with Bev's parents, Bob and Frances Poe. I had been to her home a couple of times.

As the wedding approached, there was a certain reminder that soon enough, we would be one. At least once a week I would find a special pastry in my seminary mailbox. It matched a nickname I had given her because of my appreciation for, dare I say fixation on, a certain part of her anatomy. She seemed to have a limitless supply of "Honey Buns."

As that semester came to a close, Bev headed home to Findlay to make final preparations, and I drove to Lockport, New York, where I spent several weeks being employed by the Salvation Army. I don't remember how I came upon this job, but somehow the year before, I had discovered that a limited number of bell ringers were employed on a full-time basis. The Captains, a married couple, had moved from ministry in Auburn, New York, to Lockport. It had worked so well the year before that they wanted me to come there and ring. I lived with them during those days of raising money during the Christmas season.

Thankfully, they still had a house after a rather hilarious incident. I was using the bathroom and lit a stick match to dispel the odor, when a piece flew off, igniting the fringe at the top of the shower curtain! I managed to jump up and rip the curtain down into the tub, extinguishing the flames. However, the ceiling and some of the walls were covered with soot. I was thankful, but extremely embarrassed, to explain this when the couple arrived home to find me trying to clean up the mess. I had quite a story to share with Bev later that day when we talked on the phone.

I was so glad to complete this work, stop for a couple of days at home to celebrate Christmas, and then head for Findlay. Bev's folks provided me with a room in their home for the two days between Christmas and our wedding day. Our rehearsal the night before was marked by a blood vessel popping in Bev's left eye, as well as an absent sense of humor. The rehearsal went well enough, I thought, but for some reason, when we were seated for dinner at Bill Knapp's, Bev whispered in my ear, "I guess I don't have to tell you how uptight I am!" It was all downhill from there.

The next day at one o'clock in the sanctuary of St. Mark's United Methodist Church in Findlay, Ohio, Beverly Jean Poe Davis became my wife and life's partner. Pop Harris and J. Paul Jones officiated as we exchanged vows and worshipped the Lord with carefully selected music and verse, played and sung by a small ensemble put together by some of Bev's friends.

Following the wedding, we enjoyed a cake and punch reception in the church fellowship hall. I appreciated so much my sister, Connie, and her husband, Jack, being present for the wedding and reception. My sister, Paula, was also there. My mom and dad were unable to attend because of mom's fear of driving or riding long distances in the winter.

Finally, we were off to our honeymoon destination, stopping at a family reunion on the way. We were exhausted by the time we arrived at the Sawmill Creek Resort in Huron, Ohio, on the shore of Lake Erie, near Sandusky.

We had a wonderful two-night honeymoon, wrapped in the warmth of our love for one another, surrounded by a frozen landscape, created by water surges thrown onto the shore. It was unforgettable.

Home

The First Six Months

Our life together began in earnest when we returned from our brief honeymoon on the shore of Lake Erie. We settled into our little basement apartment in Wilmore. It had been no small challenge finding a place, since it was an odd time to move, in the middle of a school year. Thankfully, Dr. George Turner, New Testament professor at Asbury Seminary, the one who requested the reading of "*How to Read a Book*," and his wife, offered their unused housing. It was perfect for us. It contained a living room/dining area, galley kitchen, bedroom and bath. Only a partial wall and curtain kept it from being one room, separated by a pass-through counter. We could almost jump from the kitchen into bed! It was so wonderful to attend our classes and then come home to each other.

I also worked at Rogers restaurant, until the end of March, when I ended my almost three-year employment. By then, a hernia that I had acquired lifting weights three years prior, had begun bothering me enough to need surgical repair. So early on, Bev's compassion, patience, and skill as a caretaker, came into play. Looking back, we laugh about certain things that had to be done and endured as I recovered.

In our spare time, we enjoyed baking bread together and learning how not to get in each other's way when getting ready for school or bed. Our little apartment became a haven for a young couple or two who needed to "escape" the strictures of the college. We would host them for dinner or just an evening watching TV, enjoying snacks and some "cuddle" time.

Also, during this time, I, in particular, began to sense more deeply what I had gotten myself into. We experienced those little aggravations and tiffs, and I was reminded that the covenant of marriage we had entered involved a lifetime of learning how to compromise and forgive.

Dr. and Mrs. Turner were gracious landlords. There were two ways to enter or leave our apartment. We always used the sliding glass door which exited onto a backyard patio. But there was also a door to a stairway leading into their home. On occasion they would invite us to use that door and join them for afternoon coffee and cookies. We discovered a gentle and caring couple who modeled a life-long partnership. Dr. Turner became more than a seminary professor who taught Inductive Bible Study and prepared us for pastoral ministry.

I completed my field ministry assignment during this time. Master of Divinity students were assigned to a church during their final year of seminary. This was to provide us with practical orientation and "hands on" experience prior to assuming the pastoral role ourselves. Barry "Praise God" Bennett and I were placed at the First United Methodist Church in Cynthiana, Kentucky. We worked with a seasoned pastor who took us on pastoral visits, invited us to sit in on various meetings, and involved us in Sunday worship, among other things. Travel to and from Cynthiana involved a fifty-mile drive each way, mainly on rural roads. Through this experience, Barry and I became good friends. He earned the moniker, "Praise God," because he loved to punctuate the conversation with "Well, Praise God, brother!" As mentioned previously, he was one of the groomsmen in our wedding.

Bev and I also became close to a young married couple about our age who were members of the congregation. Jerry and Sharon extended hospitality to us on a number of occasions. They were warm-hearted Christians who were life-long Kentuckians. Jerry had a surveying business and knew the area like the back of his hand. We loved staying overnight in their neatly appointed home. A meal prepared by Sharon was a special treat. We continued our friendship long after moving north to our first appointment.

In April of my final semester of seminary, we received the news that I was being appointed to the Arkport United Methodist Church, located in the southern tier of New York State, about sixty miles south of Rochester. We arranged a meeting with the Pastor-Parish Relations Committee so that we could introduce ourselves to some of the folks whom I would serve as pastor. Near the end of April, Bev and I traveled to Arkport, where we met with committee members in the home of Bob and Glenora Crowell. We experienced much affirmation and were assured that we would be embraced by the eighty active-members housed in a sixty-year- old brick church building, in the center of a small village of about nine hundred people. I will never forget one committee member's words to me, "We'll back you all the way."

We included in this trip, six hundred miles north from Wilmore, an interview at Houghton College. Houghton was within commuting distance of Arkport, and Bev could complete her Social Work curriculum there. It didn't strike me then, but later, I remembered that I had long ago felt impressed by the Lord that whomever I married would be a graduate of Houghton.   Following the ending of my engagement to Shelly, the Houghton student, during the first semester of my first year of seminary, I had laughed at that impression, thinking "there goes that!"   It was more than coincidental that Bev graduated from Houghton in 1978, two years after moving to Arkport.   One of my favorite hymns sums up this impression and its fulfillment: "God Moves in a Mysterious Way, His Wonders to Perform."

 Both sets of our parents came to Wilmore for my graduation from Asbury Seminary. This gave Bev's folks, Bob and Frances, the opportunity to become acquainted with my mom and dad, Sam and Evie.

We had a memorable time touring the rolling countryside, full of narrow, winding roads, and white fences, marking the perimeters of horse farms.   Probably the highlight was enjoying a graduation dinner at Shaker Town. We laughed a lot as Mom and Dad Poe got to experience firsthand the nuttiness of my parents.

As May turned into June, the reality of our first big move overtook us. I rented a U-Haul truck, and we headed to Findlay, Ohio, with me driving the truck and Bev driving her car. I had given my Mustang to my sister, Paula, since using Bev's 1960's vintage four-door Rambler seemed more practical as a family car. (This is the car referred to in my book, *Bat Tongs and Other Humorous Reflections on*  *Pastoral Ministry*, as the "Mean Green Mochine") We arrived at the Poe residence and loaded a few pieces of furniture, and other home-making items. We also intended to pick up "Nakinis Wee Tinkle," Bev's registered, runt, American Eskimo dog, whom her sister, Marcia, had been caring for. However, we thought it best to have her mom and dad bring him after we had dealt with the confusion of settling into the Arkport parsonage. Wee Tinkle was epileptic and extremely high strung.

Another stop in Jamestown, New York to pick up more furniture that I had stored at John and Charlotte Cooke's parsonage, and we were headed for our own first house. I knew that wherever the Lord would lead us, I had found a home, in the expansive love of both the Lord and my wife of six months, Beverly Jean Poe Crawford.

Postscript

That first six months, where we began to establish our home

together, initiated a forty-three year adventure which continues. The Lord has blessed Bev and me with three beautiful children, a son-in-law and daughter-in-law, and three precious grandchildren. After thirty-three years in full-time pastoral ministry in the United Methodist Church, we are now settled into retirement in Fairport, New York.

My love for my Dream Woman continues to deepen. Many times I have given thanks for listening to the still small voice which directed me towards Asbury Theological Seminary. The preparation for pastoral ministry which I received, the healing from damaged emotions I experienced, and the finding of my home in this world in Beverly Jean Poe Crawford, leave no doubt as to the ways that the Lord of all creation works out His redemptive plan.

"Now to Him who is able to do immeasurably more than all we ask or imagine, according to his power that is work within us, to him be glory in the church and in Christ Jesus throughout all generations, forever and ever! Amen."   *Ephesians 3:20-21*

About the Author

Born: August 8, 1945 in Jamestown, New York, raised in Kansas and New York, Graduated from Frewsburg Central in Chautauqua County, New York -

1963 served in the US Army as a Motion Picture Photographer from November 1964 - November 1967 Attended Jamestown Community College in 1968-69 Graduated from Houghton College in 1972 with a B.A. in Religion Graduated from Asbury Theological Seminary in 1976 with a Master of Divinity Degree-

Met my wife, Beverly, while a seminary student and we married in December 1975-

We have three beautiful children, daughter in law, son in law and three grandchildren-

Retired ten years now after serving for 33 years in full time pastoral ministry. This included five appointments Presently living in Fairport, New York.

Acknowledgment

I want to thank Julia Mattocks Wistran and Julie Ann (Hoffman) Slaby for proofreading this book. Both Julies were of inestimable help in shaping the text and facilitating my voice therein.

Julie Wistran is a retired High School English teacher who lives with her husband in Salem, Massachusetts. Julie was my next-door neighbor growing up just outside Frewsburg, New York. She holds a couple of spots in this book. Her brother, Terry, was a major source of and participant in the hijinks I describe in "Life Around the Burg."

Julie Slaby is an Instructor in the English Department of Daemen College in Amherst, New York. She lives with her husband and their new baby in Wilson, New York. Julie, with her family, the Hoffmans, were members of the congregation I served as pastor in Barker, New York. I will never forget a story Julie wrote about some junked jeeps in the woods titled "Jeep Heaven." This was a high school essay and I knew then that she had writing in her future.

Both of these Julies were generous in their praise and refused to allow me to compensate them.

Jeff Crawford

All the books by the author are available on Amazon.com and Barns and Nobel Online.

This book is about the laughter and dancing "seasons." Oh, how we need to find the humor in life. It is my hope that these reflections will help the reader discover or rediscover this dynamic! May you laugh and be thankful to our Gracious God as you are reminded of the imperfections that permeate us all. "ISBN-13: 978-1978399938

ISBN-10: 1978399936

Up and coming:

Chasing Golf

Talk to the author:

Email: blumoonjman60@yahoo.com

Made in the USA
Middletown, DE
03 November 2019